Don't Lose Heart!
A Widow's Guide to Growing Stronger

By:

Mary Beth Woll, MA, LMHC
Linda Smith
Paul Meier, MD

Endorsements

In 2015, I co-authored *"Growing Stronger: 12 Guidelines to Turn Your Darkest Hour into Your Greatest Victory"* with Meier Clinic therapist Mary Beth Woll. Our desire was to offer the Church a resource to bring hope and help to women suffering from crises, trauma, depression, or grief.

Four short years later, Mary Beth suffered the greatest trauma and grief of her life when she was suddenly widowed by the loss of Bob, her dear husband of 39 years. After navigating the first devastating almost year and a half without Bob, Mary Beth and teacher/mentor Linda Smith (also a widow) revised and adapted "Growing Stronger" especially for the needs of widows.

As Founder of the national chain of Meier Clinics, I recommend *Don't Lose Heart!* as a group or individual study for widows as written by two women who really understand and can relate to their pain.

Paul Meier, MD
Founder of the National Chain of Meier Clinics

On the spectrum of human emotions, grief has to be one of the deepest and most painful to navigate. The loss of a husband releases a gamut of feelings from sorrow, to anger, to despair, to hopelessness. You are thrust into a world you never wanted or expected. The smallest, seemingly insignificant thing can trigger a torrent of tears. It can be scary, lonely, confusing, and overwhelming as you learn to live life without the love of your life.

We were not meant to walk this dark valley by ourselves. Caring support from those who have "been there," can be a ray of hope to the hurting heart. The co-authors, Mary Beth Woll and Linda Smith, are two such people. Having walked their own grief journeys, they now provide loving support for those who find themselves in the throes of widowhood. Based on their wealth of experience and training, the book you are holding contains godly wisdom as well as practical helps to guide you through your own grief process. You will be encouraged, strengthened, and inspired to keep putting one foot in front of the other, one day at a time...sometimes even one minute at a time...so that you don't lose heart.

Rev. Diane Fink
Sonrise Christian Center, Everett, WA
CCF Ministries, Lowell, MS

Endorsements

"For many years I have had a deep concern for ministry widows! Who cares for them and helps them through the process? On September 11, 2019, I became a widow after 48 years of marriage and came to the realization that there is very little support for widows in ministry. I believe the book *"Don't Lose Heart!"* is an absolute must read and "work through" to be a map in the "uncharted wilderness" of widowhood.

After becoming a widow, there were no "widow mentors" to help me along the way for the first nine months until Mary Beth and Linda extended comforting support. I am so grateful to God for their lives and loving support that has helped me immensely in the "grief journey". In Mexico alone, there have been over 1,000 pastors that have died during the "Covid-19 crisis." I highly recommend working through the questions in this book, as grief is real, exhausting and challenging."

Ruth Martinez (Ost)
Bible Teacher and Conference Speaker
Instituto Ministerial El Calvario
Master's Resourcing Commission

As I was reviewing Don't Lose Heart! these are some words that I felt reflected the message contained in its pages. Words like truthful, biblical, transparent, honest, encouraging, hopeful and very practical.

There is no doubt that *Don't Lose Heart!* will certainly be of great help and encouragement to women going through a time of transition to embracing the "new normal" of being a widow. Mary Beth Woll, Linda Smith, and Dr. Paul Meier have done an excellent job of providing understanding, compassion and truth in this book. Their book is a "must read" for any women needing help with transition at this time in their lives.

For my wife Faith and I, this book has special meaning since we, along with many others, were able to "be there" for Mary Beth during those early days of transition at the time of the loss of her husband Bob. We are so happy to see all the progress she has made. She has turned her loss into a blessing for many others.

Rev. Doug Martin
Associate Pastor/Elder
Sonrise Christian Center

Endorsements

Drawing on the searing pain and loss of widowhood, Mary Beth Woll and Linda Smith offer a practical handbook of hope and healing for those who grieve. Their experiences and devotion to the Lord, coupled with the remarkable, decades-long ministry of Dr. Paul Meier, provide a solidly biblical and compassionate pathway for the new widow, and an effective tool for those who would work with them in a small-group setting. With carefully crafted discussion questions, insightful understanding of the scriptures, and the goal of putting God first, *Don't Lose Heart!* should rest on every widow's bookshelf.

Carolyn Underhill, Pastor's wife
Women's Ministry Director
Teacher of "Grace-Notes", a Bible class designed for
women who attend church alone

It is with great appreciation that I would recommend you read this book(let) prayerfully, especially if you are now a widow or a person going through profound grief.

Mary Beth has been through the "fire" of widowhood. She has depended on the Lord, and is honoring Him as she now in turn wants to comfort others as she was comforted.

It is out of a broken heart, (which the Lord has been restoring since the month of June 2019, when her special husband and brother in the Lord, Bob, went on to his "eternal reward") that she has sought to make available to others the resources, and with a giving heart, desired that all those who weep will be comforted. It is through this brokenness that she has permitted the light of Jesus in her to shine forth to a hurting world, and spiritual family members in need, as she has sought to be a faithful servant.

I had known Bob and Mary Beth from Bible School days in the early 70's, but got close to them via the internet at a very crucial moment, during the last few months before the Lord called her Bob home to glory. Our churches in Dieppe and Paris, France, have often been rescue stations for the broken-hearted, and the Lord has always given us the Promises in His Word, and the mission to go forth in His anointing, to see those hearts healed!

Rev. Mark Ost
Pastor at Faith, Hope and Love Church
Greater Paris Metropolitan Region

Endorsements

Walking with Mary Beth Woll over the years has been a wonderful journey as she has processed her trauma. This past year, as Mary Beth moved through her grief at the loss of her husband, has been eye opening. She has really explored the unique trauma of a widow's grief. I commend Mary Beth and her desire to bring relief to the world of acute grief of widowhood. I know that as you read this book and explore the messages/exercises and words of wisdom, you will find a way to navigate your own grief and help others.

Lilla Collingridge Marie, LMHC
Director and Therapist
Meier Clinics

When my husband J.R. went to be with the Lord in May of 2018, I began an experience of grief that no other loss in my life had prepared me for. It affected everything in my life and filled me, all day long sometimes, with a strange feeling in my bones like the glow of a fever. It affected my physical health so that my immune system was weakened for the first year. Grief distracted me so that I sometimes did dumb things- like once I drove straight through the arm of a toll booth without realizing it before I broke through it! Grief humbled me and made me positive that I needed help to survive this journey down the valley of the shadow of death.

That's why I was thrilled to be invited by my friend Ruth Martinez to join an on line Grief Share group with Mary Beth Woll and Linda Smith. This has been a sweet experience of fellowship with other widowed women in the ministry. It's so comforting to know that they are experiencing the same type of loss. I learn so much from each of them as they share how the Lord is comforting them and helping them grow stronger.

How glad I am to recommend Woll and Smith's new book, *Don't Lose Heart!,* with its powerful and nourishing themes inspired by Hebrews Chapter 12. The great cloud of witnesses is cheering us on! With the nourishment of God's Word, and the loving encouragement of other believing widows, we can run our race! Love in Jesus,

Nancy Honeytree Miller
Singer/Songwriter

Endorsements

We are living in an age and a culture where youthfulness is prized and those with life-experience are jettisoned, especially those marked by personal loss, like the widow. The result is a generation of spiritually orphaned young people without an anchor or help. But I believe God is turning this unfortunate trend around. He is turning the hearts of the fathers and mothers of the faith to the children and the children to their spiritual fathers and mothers (Malachi 4:6). And for this the Church needs healthy, healed widows.

There is very little in life as important as being needed and having a place from which to help others in their journey. The authors of *Don't Lose Heart!* do an amazing job of providing that hope and that place of healing for widows to be able to move beyond their loss and not just to bring comfort to others (2 Corinthians 1:4) but invest in future generations.

It is my privilege to endorse *Don't Lose Heart!*, and recommend it not only for the benefit of the content but as a study, guiding small groups in the healing process.

Dr. Alec E. Rowlands
Senior Pastor: Westgate Chapel
Founder: Church Awakening

Having been married forty-eight years and friends for fifty-one, Kay and I cannot imagine the massive vacuum that will be created on that inevitable day when one of us will lose the other. The trauma created by the sudden or gradual loss of a life partner is earth shattering. When we together becomes a me alone, we are suddenly shocked, paralyzed and horribly disoriented. Grief becomes all consuming. At some point, when the mourner begins to emerge from the fog, *Don't Loose Heart!* will become a helpful companion on the journey of grief recovery.

Milan Yerkovich
Co-author, How We Love, How We Love Workbook,
How We Love our Kids (www.howwelove.com)
Co-host New Life Live Radio (www.newlife.com)
Founder Relationship 180 counseling center
(www.relationship180.com).

ISBN paperback: 978-1-7362169-0-3
ISBN eBook: 978-1-7362169-1-0

Cover Design by: David Woll
Interior Layout/ Self-Publishing by: Kristi Knowles

DON'T LOSE *heart!*

A WIDOW'S GUIDE TO GROWING STRONGER

BY MARY BETH WOLL, MA, LMHC,
LINDA SMITH, & PAUL MEIER, MD

Dedication

In loving memory of
Kirby Smith and Bob Woll
who finished their races first
and are now cheering us on from that
"great cloud of witnesses".

We're running as fast as we can!
We'll see you at the finish line!

Love,
Linda and Mary Beth

Acknowledgements

To Kristi Knowles, our editor/publisher extraordinaire, we owe a huge debt of thanks and many hugs!

Many thanks to David Woll, our graphic artist, who through his expertise captured our hearts' vision and translated it into our beautiful cover.

Much gratitude to Rolland Wright for his expert leadership. He has been inspirational and empowering.

Special thanks to Officer Nathan Romaneschi of the Washington State Patrol who sped us on our way. We were working on Chapter Two when we met. Thank you, Sir!

Contents

Foreword

It is an honor and complete joy to introduce Mary Beth Woll and Linda Smith to widows worldwide. It is so fulfilling to watch people who discover their **"do"**—to heal, flourish, grow and walk in courage and confidence.

They will mentor you if you will engage. They will hold you up if you are weak. Their words of wisdom are filled with compassion and understanding.

Together, they are walking the path of widowhood. Together they are processing their grief. Together they are sharing the keys to processing grief and pursuing wholeness.

These are not empty words. Their insights are born from an especially deep bond. Mary Beth and Linda have been friends for years. Linda's husband Kirby passed six years before Mary Beth's Robert (Bob). It is Linda who has mentored Mary Beth. Both recognize the providential hand of God in Linda being there for Mary Beth. They now walk the ministry journey together mentoring others in their season of grief.

It was a recent ministry trip to Columbia Falls, Montana, in the fall of 2020, that I attribute as the catalyst that ignited our two co-authors. They drove back from Montana inspired with a vision to help other widows in the grieving process. Two chapters were written between Spokane and home. The balance of the book was accomplished over the next couple of weeks. Other grief resources have been born out of that trip.

In **Don't Lose Heart!**, they share their hearts with a compassion that only those who have walked this path can understand. They minister with 2 Cor.1: 3-7 conviction, compelled to provide comfort as they have been comforted. **If you are a widow, this book will encourage you. If you are a widow, they share in your suffering.**

Our hope is that the book you hold in your hands will help you and other widows worldwide heal emotionally, and once healed, empower you to pass the comfort you receive on to other widows. Your compassion then overflows to others who are grieving the loss of their spouse. You too can transition into a life of ministry to those who are freshly walking where you have been. **Will you consider walking alongside widows with the help of The Widows Project?**

By engaging in the process of comforting others, you will gain a renewed purpose and zeal for living.

- Rolland Wright, Founder of The Widows Project

THE Widows PROJECT

The Widows Project is a faith-based organization founded in 2015 and located in Everett, Washington. We are focused on creating resources that help the widowed process their grief, regain balance, and embrace a new lifestyle of hope and optimism, to move them from hopelessness and despair to wholeness.

For more information or to donate, please visit:
www.thewidowsproject.org

Find us on Facebook at:
The Widows Project

Rolland Wright:

Rolland Wright is the President and Founder of **The Widows Project**. He founded this organization in 2015 to assist churches and local organizations to better serve widows. He holds a bachelor's degree from Biola University. His deep compassion for the hurting compelled him to write: "*The Widows Project: Serving the Widowed with the Father's Heart.*"

Welcome to Don't Lose Heart!

Don't Lose Heart! has a very definite purpose and goal—to give widows healing support during their grieving process. We want to help them recover from their devastating loss so they can move forward into a life of effectiveness for God, becoming fruitful; even 30, 60, and 100 times more productive than ever before! (Mark 4:20)

As a therapist (Mary Beth Woll, MA, LMHC) and a psychiatrist (Paul Meier, MD), we love helping people during those tough times, and have devoted our careers to doing so. We love our jobs because it brings such great joy to help others. The following pages offer a glimpse into the vision the Lord has given us through years of counseling ministry, as well as Mary Beth's personal journey of grief and loss following the passing of Bob, her husband of 39 years.

Linda Smith is a seasoned widow of seven years who mentored Mary Beth and loved her through the earliest and darkest days of widowhood. With a background in Christian Education and church ministry, Linda has also mentored many other women through small groups, individual mentoring, and prayer support.

God has impressed upon us the need for the local church to provide a haven for widows. Unfortunately, many churches are not prepared to offer this kind of support. Although nobody wants it to happen, widows often fall through the cracks of the church structure. Sometimes church members don't know how to reach out, and the church staff may feel overwhelmed by their needs.

Rolland Wright also noticed a need for the local church to provide critical emotional support for women suffering the greatest loss of their lives. In response, in 2015 he founded The Widows Project and wrote a book about his vision: *The Widows Project: Serving the Widowed with the Father's Heart.* Rolland's key ministry verse is James 1:27, "Religion that God our Father accepts as pure and faultless is this: to look after orphans and widows in their distress and to keep oneself from being polluted by the world."

This book is our collective response to the needs of widows everywhere. We have designed this book to be used in a small group setting, following the 13-week GriefShare program. While GriefShare serves well people suffering the loss of loved ones, the 12-week course of *Don't Lose Heart!* is written to address the unique pain and specific needs of widows. It can, however, stand alone as a resource for individuals.

We hope that this book will ease your grief and that you will pass it on to another widow in need of the comfort you have received from *Don't Lose Heart!*. May God bless you as you follow Him through this especially important journey!

Mary Beth Woll, MA, LMHC
Therapist
Meier Clinics

Linda Smith

Paul Meier, MD
Founder of the National Chain of
Meier Clinics

DON'T LOSE *heart!*

A WIDOW'S GUIDE TO GROWING STRONGER

BY MARY BETH WOLL, MA, LMHC, LINDA SMITH, & PAUL MEIER, MD

Growing Stronger Guideline #1
KEEP FIRST THINGS FIRST

Develop an intimate relationship with Jesus because you are **powerless** to overcome **grief** in your own strength.

CHAPTER ONE

KEEP FIRST THINGS FIRST
PREACH THE GOOD NEWS TO THE POOR

"The Spirit of the Sovereign Lord is on me, because the Lord has anointed me to preach good news to the poor" (Isaiah 61:1, NIV).

This beautiful scripture in Isaiah 61:1–4 describes Jesus' mission to those in need. Jesus read this aloud in the Synagogue, as recorded in Luke 4. His ministry, outlined in these verses, inspired us, Christian therapist Mary Beth Woll, Christian psychiatrist Paul Meier, and Christian teacher/mentor Linda Smith, to write this book. Isaiah 61:1–4, along with Hebrews 12:1–13 and the Guidelines that emerged from them, express the special love and passion we have to help widows.

Who are "The Poor?"
While the term "poor" can refer to those in financial need, it also describes those who are poor in spirit—emotionally and spiritually—regardless of their financial status. This is the same word that Jesus used in the Sermon on the Mount when He said, "Blessed are the poor in spirit, for theirs is the Kingdom of Heaven" (Matt. 5:3). But the "Kingdom of Heaven" not only refers to that eternal and perfect place where God exists, but a new life that begins now when we turn ourselves over to God. We all come to a point when we realize that we have a need and are powerless to meet it in our own strength—in other words, we are poor in spirit. That is when we are most ready to receive the Gospel—the Good News—and ask Jesus to help us! He hears our cry for help and opens the way to new and wonderful possibilities. We choose to live His way by His power working in and through us.

First Things First
Some of you reading this already know Jesus personally and are seeking to develop a deeper level of intimacy with Him. You know that you are on your way to Heaven, but you need His wisdom and strength to get through your grief. You know that when you have Jesus, you have all you need. Romans 8:32 (NLT) reminds us, "Since He did not spare even His own Son, but gave Him up for us all, won't He also give us everything else?"

Others of you do not yet have a personal relationship with Jesus.

You may ask, "How can I know Jesus, too?"

One way to enter into a personal relationship with Jesus is to follow "The Romans Road." Anyone can start on this life-changing journey with Him by understanding and acting on these basic biblical truths:

- **We are all sinners in need of a Savior.** Romans 3:23 says, "For all have sinned and fall short of the glory of God."
- **Without Jesus, we are separated from God, now and in the afterlife.** Romans 6:23a says, "For the wages of sin is death..."
- **But with Jesus, we can have eternal life, beginning right now.** Romans 6:23b says, "...but the gift of God is eternal life in Christ Jesus our Lord."

So, you may ask, "What must one do to have this eternal life with Jesus?" Romans 10:9–10 explains:

That if you confess with your mouth, "Jesus is Lord," and believe in your heart that God raised Him from the dead, you will be saved. For it is with your heart that you believe and are justified, and it is with your mouth that you confess and are saved.

Trust God to forgive your sins and enter your life. He is offering this to you as a free gift. You can't earn it.

If you are ready to enter into a personal relationship with Jesus, you can pray this prayer:

Jesus, You and I both know that I have committed sins in my life—done things at times that have hurt You and others. I believe You died on the cross and rose to life again to pay for my sins. I ask You right now to come into my heart and become the Lord of my life. Forgive me for the sins I have committed in the past or may commit in the future. Amen.

If you have just prayed this prayer for the first time, God says that you are born again and on your way to Heaven.

Here-and-Now Help with a Heavenly Perspective

As a widow thinks about Heaven, she often wonders what her relationship to her husband will be like when all the believers join those already in Heaven. After all, we were each made by God to love and be loved. That is a basic desire for us here on earth. Many of us experienced the highest expression of love through the sexual relationship with our husbands. It was so intimate, satisfying, and central to our marriages.

God created marriage for us "in the beginning." In intimacy and commitment, husband and wife become one. That is a mystery we cannot understand. Likewise, we cannot explain the way that God is like a Bridegroom and the Church of Jesus like His Bride. This is love at its best, beyond our comprehension. Revelation 21:4 tells us that, "He will wipe away every tear from their eyes, and there will be no more death or sorrow or crying or pain. All these things are gone forever." Would our marriages fit into Heaven's experience? We may have enjoyed great marriages, by earthly standards, but Heaven's love is perfect.

Jesus explained to His disciples that He was going away to prepare Heaven for us, and He will come and get us at just the right time. He came for our husbands at just the right time, too. John 14:1 (NLT) says, "Don't let your hearts be troubled. Trust God and trust also in Me." Why? Because Heavenly love will far supersede all earthly expressions and experiences. God's love is beyond imagination. We cannot fathom it now, even if Christ were to give us all the details. Paul alludes to this in 1 Corinthians 2:9. "No eye has seen, nor ear has heard, and no mind has imagined what God has prepared for those who love Him." The great love we have experienced on earth is just a shadow of what we will find when we get to Heaven and live in perfect love.

Discussion Questions

1. Have you ever received Jesus as your Savior? If so, please share that experience with the group. Some know they have done so, but do not remember the specific moment when they began their relationship with God. Others experienced a distinct encounter with God when they first trusted Jesus.

   Dr. Meier gave his heart to Jesus in his Sunday School class when he was six years old but rededicated his life in a more meaningful way at age 16.

   At age 5, Mary Beth tearfully confessed to her mother that she had lied to her about something. Her mother forgave her and then wisely reminded, "There's Someone else you need to tell that you are sorry: God." Then she led Mary Beth in a prayer to ask Jesus to forgive her and to come into her heart. As Mary Beth grew, so did her faith in God and deep personal relationship with Him.

Linda was so young when she came to know Jesus that she remembers a series of commitments and recommitments to Him as she matured.

Everyone's moment of introduction to Jesus as Lord and Savior is unique, so we hope you will share your own personal experience with others.

_____

_____

_____

_____

_____

_____

_____

2. If you have not yet received Christ, would you describe yourself as (a) still contemplating the decision, (b) having some questions about receiving Christ, or (c) not yet ready?

_____

_____

_____

_____

_____

_____

_____

_____

3. If you replied to the previous question with answer "a" or "b," your group leader or a pastor will be happy to discuss any questions you may have.

    As with any big decision, it is wise to get counsel. If you are ready, and would like to know Jesus personally right now, then sincerely pray this prayer:

> Jesus, You and I both know that I have committed sins in my life—done things at times that have hurt You and others. I believe You died on the cross and rose to life again to pay for my sins. I ask You right now to come into my heart and become the Lord of my life. Forgive me for the sins I have committed in the past or may commit in the future. Amen.

Growing Stronger Guideline #2

DON'T SUFFER ALONE

Give your broken heart to God and His people to
receive healing from both.

Chapter Two
Don't Suffer Alone
Bind Up the Brokenhearted

"The Spirit of the Sovereign Lord is on me...He has sent me to bind up the brokenhearted" (Isaiah 61:1).

Beginning the Healing Process

In medical school, we learned that if you break your arm and it heals properly, that part of your arm will be stronger than the rest of it. If you were to break that arm again in a future accident, it would not break where it had previously healed. In the same way, a broken heart can be painful. Nearly all of us have felt this ache at one time or another, but, as God heals our broken hearts, in the end He makes us stronger than we ever were before.

Don't Suffer Alone

After establishing an intimate relationship with Jesus, we move on, through our loneliness, to our second Guideline. Here, we bring our broken hearts to God and His loving people, our spiritual brothers and sisters. We can share our aching souls with a trusted friend or relative, a pastor, counselor, or grief group.

A shared burden becomes a half burden. Simply telling your grief story to God and one or more caring persons will likely relieve a great deal of your pain. Consider finding a trusted widow who has already worked through her grief and can mentor you through your grief. As you share your feelings of sorrow and loss, she will identify with you. She has been there and has already walked this road. She will recognize the "valley of the shadow of death" and help to guide you through it. She will not be scared by your intense emotions because she has experienced them, too. Although each widow has her unique grief experience, there will be many commonalities with which she will be able to relate. As you share and pray, God will guide you together toward healing.

Someone with a healed heart often responds by passing on to others the renewal that they have received. But healing is a process, as reflected in our Twelve Guidelines. The first two Guidelines are the most important and necessary steps. First, trust Jesus for love, support, and guidance, then second, take your broken heart and burdens to Him and significant others.

As you begin to recover, 1 Peter 5:10 affirms, God will *"personally come and pick you up, and set you firmly in place, and make you stronger than ever" (TLB).*

Jesus Heals Broken Hearts

Jesus considers mending broken hearts to be critical, second only to preaching the Gospel. In fact, Jesus said that the whole Law can be summed up in two commands: first, "Love the Lord your God with all your heart and with all your soul and with all your strength and with all your mind," and second, "Love your neighbor as yourself" (Luke 10:27). To illustrate loving our neighbor, Jesus tells the parable of the Good Samaritan (Luke 10:25–37). Let's look at this story together and reflect on the actions of the individual characters.

The Wounded Person

The wounded person is not usually the focus of this story, but because of her devasting loss, the widow may best relate to this character. Severely beaten, the wounded man was left for half dead. Because a husband and wife become one, when a woman loses her husband, she may feel that half of herself has died. Research shows that "people whose spouses have just died have a whopping 66% increased chance of dying themselves within the first three months following their spouse's death." (Leonard Holmes) This is called the "Widowhood Effect." In fact, the widow who had a close relationship with her husband is at greater risk for depression following his passing. Like the wounded man, the widow's circumstances may render her useless and in desperate need of assistance. She may even be temporarily non-functional and dependent on the kindness and care of others.

God recognizes the helpless state of the widow. He reminds us that, "Pure and genuine religion in the sight of God the Father means caring for orphans and widows in their distress" (James 1:27, NLT).

The Priest and the Levite

The wounded person may have expected the priest or the Levite to be the first to respond. Similarly, new widows are often surprised by who does or does not notice their woundedness. We do not know why the priest and the Levite didn't stop, but we see that God unexpectedly provided for the wounded man from an unlikely source—a Samaritan!

The Good Samaritan

The Good Samaritan saw the state of the wounded man, and unlike the priest and the Levite who passed by on the other side of the road, he felt sympathy for him. The Samaritan was also traveling, but he responded compassionately when he came upon the wounded man. He allowed his compassion to move him into action. He needed to move the wounded man off the dangerous road and into a safe place where he could recuperate. Similarly, widows may need a safe haven in which to recover. For some, that may just be a listening ear or someone to hold her while she cries.

The Good Samaritan treated the man's wounds with oil and wine, a kind of ancient first aid which supplied soothing and antiseptic properties. When Jesus binds up the widow's broken heart, He sometimes uses others to apply the "oil" of grace to soothe her soul and the "wine" of truth to cleanse the wound. We need to receive both grace and truth from God and others in order to heal properly.

After my (Mary Beth's) husband Bob died, I was temporarily incapacitated. Not only was I suffering from grief and loss, but I was physically depleted as well. Because of my fierce devotion to Bob and unwillingness to leave his side during his intense illness and hospitalization, I suffered from sleep deprivation and life-threatening anemia. My adult children were also suffering great loss and caring for their own children who were missing their Papa Bob.

Family, friends, neighbors, and church staff lovingly gave of their time, money, service and energy, but I needed extended care to heal—body, soul and spirit. A friend I had known for over 40 years, resurfaced in my life. Linda Smith had lost her dear husband Kirby six years prior. She knew the grief road that lay ahead of me. At Bob's memorial service, Linda walked up to me, looked me squarely in the eye and said, "We're going to be good friends again."

I knew, at that moment, that God was speaking to me through Linda. Little did I know that I would live with Linda for three and a half months while she took care of me. I was physically disabled and emotionally devastated. I experienced the severe emotional pain of deep grief and loss. I was the wounded person in this scenario. Like the Good Samaritan, Linda took care of me until I could return home.

The Innkeeper

The Good Samaritan couldn't do it all by himself. The wounded man needed more help than one person could provide. Similarly, there may already be established resources for the widow, but, like the wounded man, she may be too disoriented and need help to make those connections. There is a gap between the time the casseroles stop coming and when she can function, where the widow will need help, sometimes even with daily chores.

Dear widow, we have good news for you. Although your world may have come crashing down when your husband died, there are people still standing on their feet – people who are functioning well. The gift of service (or helps) is a spiritual gift that some people use on a regular basis. They love to help. They are gifted helpers. Others will take up the role of helping because they care about you and want to bless you. It's scriptural. There would have been no Good Samaritan if there hadn't been a man down. Lazarus would not have been raised from the dead if Jesus had not responded to Mary and Martha's cry for help. In prison, Paul needed his coat for warmth and his parchments so he could write the Pauline epistles for us.

There are also people who like to organize help. Let them. Let me. I (Linda) would suggest that you (or your helper) get two pieces of paper. On one piece, make a list of what needs to be done and the deadline if there is one. On the other piece of paper, write down the names of people who offered to help – even the ones who said, "Let me know if you need anything." Add contact information so you can follow up easily. Then match up the needs with the helpers.

For the first two weeks (at least) after your husband's death, have an organizer/administrator stay with you – someone who knows how to get things done. It's another gift. Grief requires so much time, energy, and attention. You can't do it all alone. God gave us friends and family to help us walk through this difficult time. Don't expect your children to meet all your needs. They are grieving too. The good news is that other people want to help you. Let them.

After your helpers have gone home, you may find it useful to organize yourself in the evening for the next morning. Stand in front of the mirror and look at yourself. Ask that person in the mirror what you could do for her to show her kindness. "Do you need to take a walk?" Ask her what tasks she needs to do tomorrow. "Do you need help with housework?" Write these things down on a list. This will help her get started with her day the following morning. Many widows have a hard time with mornings. Having a plan is helpful.

The story of the Good Samaritan implies that the wounded man eventually recovered and left the inn to return home. The whole point of bearing one another's burdens is to come alongside each other during those times when we are not able to bear it alone. But after a season of recovery, we will be able, with God's help, to return to a life of fruitfulness stronger than ever before.

16

Discussion Questions

1. Sometimes grief can "ambush" us, as in the case of the wounded man, in such a way that we are not even able to ask for help. In such times of need, we must rely on the strength and goodness of others. Have you ever experienced such a time? How did others help you?

_____

_____

_____

_____

_____

_____

_____

_____

_____

2. Other times, we are able to ask for help, although it may be difficult to do so. Read Galatians 6:2–5. When are others to help us carry our burdens, and when are we to carry our own load?

    These verses sound contradictory in English versions of the Bible. In one verse we are told to bear our own burdens. In another verse of the very same passage, we are told to bear each other's burdens to fulfill the law of Christ. A contradiction? No. In the original Greek, these verses are much more understandable. What they are saying is that we should all bear our normal emotional loads. We should not depend on others for things we are fully capable of handling ourselves. Instead, we should bear each other's "overburdens" to fulfill the law of Christ.

    If you were going with friends on a camping trip, you would each carry your own backpack. It would be considered lazy and dependent to expect someone else to carry her backpack and yours as well, but the camp cook may need to carry the extra weight of pots and pans. In that case, the rest of the group should pitch in to help carry her overload and fulfill the law of Christ.

    When you come to a friend with your grief, broken spirit, and overwhelming burden, you are doing the right thing! You are also giving others the wonderful experience of helping you heal and grow emotionally and spiritually. When you become strong, you will be delighted to bear the overburdens of others as well.

_____

_____

_____

_____

_____

_____

_____

_____

3. Each one of us could easily play the part of any person in the parable. With which of these people do you most identify right now and why?

_____

_____

_____

_____

_____

_____

_____

_____

_____

_____

_____

_____

_____

4. The responses of the priest and Levite seem surprising, given that they were "in the ministry" of their day. Are there people in your life who you thought would help you and they did not? Can you imagine any reason why they didn't help you? Take a moment now to forgive them for not helping you in your time of great need.

_____

_____

_____

_____

_____

_____

_____

_____

5. At the end of the parable, Jesus tells us, "Go and do likewise" (Luke 10:37). There is a time to receive ministry from others and a time to give as well. Describe when you, or someone you love, have been "the brokenhearted." Describe when you have been the one who came alongside to help.

_____

_____

_____

_____

_____

_____

_____

_____

_____

_____

_____

Shortly after Mary Beth's husband Bob died, the Lord showed her a picture of her heart, which appeared to have exploded into smithereens.

When God healed her broken heart, He gathered up all the fragmented pieces, fit them back together again, and made something new and beautiful.

Psalm 147: 3 "He heals the brokenhearted, binding up their wounds" (NLT).

Growing Stronger Guideline #3

CONNECTION LEADS TO FREEDOM

To become truly healed, share your story with safe,
significant others as well as with Jesus.

CHAPTER THREE

CONNECTION LEADS TO FREEDOM
PROCLAIM FREEDOM FOR THE CAPTIVES

*"The Spirit of the Sovereign Lord is on me ... to proclaim
freedom for the captives and release from darkness
for the prisoners" (Isaiah 61:1).*

Jesus has come to proclaim freedom for the captives and a release from darkness for the prisoners! What wonderful news! We have talked about freedom from sin, but what exactly does it mean for the widow to be free from the dark prison of grief?

Freedom from Slavery to Grief

Sometimes people need others to help them see the way through grief. At first, the widow feels like a slave to grief, feels that grief will never end, and that she will never experience love and joy again. But others who have already traveled the grief journey can assure the new widow that there is hope. They have found freedom, and she will too! This creates a wonderful ripple effect not only for the widow, but for the lives of generations that follow!

Harriet Tubman is a great example of this type of ripple effect. A devout Christian and hero from the pre-Civil War days, Harriet was personally responsible for leading hundreds of American slaves to freedom. Born into slavery around 1820 (she did not know her exact date of birth), Harriet escaped from slavery in 1849 and returned many times to rescue family members and others who were not yet free. She developed what was called "The Underground Railroad," an elaborate system of secret safe houses organized to smuggle slaves from the South to freedom in the North *(Harriet Tubman Biography n.d.)*.

Before her escape, Harriet said, "I had reasoned this out in my mind: there was one of two things I had a right to, liberty or death; if I could not have one, I would have the other" (Tubman). She later described her experience of escaping slavery as "glorious!" "When I found I had crossed that line, I looked at my hands to see if I was the same person. There was such a glory over everything; the sun came like gold through the trees and over the fields, and I felt like I was in Heaven."

But enjoying this freedom was not enough for Harriet. She was alone in this free land and wanted to share it with others. "I had crossed the line of which I had so long been dreaming. I was free, but there was no one to welcome me to the land of freedom; I was a stranger in a strange land."

Though she was not physically strong, having suffered permanent damage from severe beatings and abuse as a slave, Harriet was courageous and indomitable. This modern-day Moses endured severe perils and hardships to bring others to freedom. William H. Seward said of her, "I have known her long, and a nobler, higher spirit, or a truer, seldom dwells in the human form."

In bringing many slaves to freedom, Harriet bravely vowed:

> But to this solemn resolution I came: I was free, and they should be free also; I would make a home for them in the North, and the Lord helping me, I would bring them all there. Oh, how I prayed then, lying all alone on de cold, damp ground. 'Oh, dear Lord,' I said, 'I ain't got no friend but You. Come to my help, Lord, for I'm in trouble!'

And help He did, indeed, as she led hundreds of slaves to freedom. Harriet rejoiced in this victory when she said, "I was the conductor of the Underground Railroad for eight years, and I can say what most conductors can't say; I never ran my train off the track and I never lost a passenger."

Surprisingly, there were some American slaves who chose to remain in bondage. In a similar way, we widows have a choice. Will we choose to stay in our grief, or to process our loss? Whether we are brand new widows or have been widows for a while, we all, from time to time, need to check our habits and mindsets. Are they moving us forward, or keeping us in bondage to grief?

Moving toward Freedom

Like Harriet Tubman, God used Moses to deliver his people from slavery in Egypt. In the desert, the people complained loudly against God and Moses. They mumbled about the manna, they complained about the quail, they whined about no water and they wanted to go back to slavery in Egypt. Some even wished they were dead. They lost sight of their destination—the Promised Land. They made choices based on how they felt, rather than remembering God's plan for them.

A widow can do the same. She can choose to reengage in life, or she can refuse freedom by making poor choices to numb her pain. While providing short-term relief, busyness, overeating, excess shopping, sex, drugs, and alcohol, and even remarrying too soon will hurt you. As 1 Timothy 5:5 says, "But the widow who lives for pleasure is dead even while she lives." These behaviors can also complicate grief and delay recovery.

But there are other more subtle mindsets that can also hinder the grieving process. Such thinking habits as self-pity, prolonged anger, and avoiding or ignoring a grief reaction instead of facing it are sometimes harder to detect. In such situations, a widow may need professional help.

Getting Connected

In some cases, delays in processing grief are beyond our control. Such distractions as one's own health, raising children, work demands, and financial concerns can so preoccupy our thoughts that there seems to be no bandwidth for grieving. But we still need God and others to gain our freedom from the slavery to grief. When a woman experiences the devastating loss of her husband, she can choose to isolate or connect with others. Every time she shares her grief story with safe people, this connection moves her forward, closer to freedom.

I (Linda) was married to Kirby Smith in April of 1976. We moved to Seattle shortly thereafter, got jobs, and started a family. We had two children, Wendy and Tyler. In 2010, Kirby was diagnosed with Chronic Lymphocytic Leukemia (CLL). Wendy married Cameron and had two little boys, Caz and Kayson, whom we loved dearly. Wendy and the boys used to come to visit every Wednesday. It was the highlight of our week.

In 2012, Kirby chose to endure chemotherapy in order to extend his life. He did not want to leave Caz, Kayson, and me behind. He acknowledged his love for our kids, but concluded that we were done raising them. Tyler had recommitted his life to Christ in 2009 and was rapidly maturing spiritually. Wendy and Cameron were spiritually solid. Praise God!

In January 2013, Tyler introduced us to the love of his life, Subha. She came to visit for New Year's Day, and we loved her immediately. She got to know Kirby at his best.

Later in the month, I was diagnosed with serious atrial fibrillation and was told I would need surgery to correct it. The surgery was scheduled for April 10.

In March of 2013, Kirby took sick. I begged him to go to the doctor but having previously overcome so many CLL ups and downs, he didn't recognize the seriousness of his illness until it was too late. Wendy and Cameron and local family and friends gathered with me by his hospital bedside, day after day, praying and hoping for healing—but that was not to be.

Tyler and Subha came from California to visit Kirby in the hospital. Tyler poured out his heart to Kirby and thanked God for giving him such a wonderful, spiritual dad. Kirby prayed a blessing over Tyler and Subha, then they had to say their goodbyes and return to California. That was the last time they saw him.

My mom and dad had planned to come from Minnesota to care for me after my April 10th heart surgery, but surgery had to be postponed. They came instead to help me lay my sweet husband to rest. In the early hours of April 16, 2013, Kirby went to be with the Lord.

Words cannot express the loss that I felt as we left the hospital without my dear husband. Even though I would continue to be surrounded by family and friends, it didn't seem possible that I could go on without the love of my life. I couldn't see past this day to freedom from grief.

My family has our own personal chaplains, my parents, Rev. Virgil and Ruth Rasmussen. It was so comforting to have them present with me and for me. They were so helpful and in tune with my needs. They returned to Seattle in May for my heart surgery – once again a huge blessing. This time, they stayed for three weeks!

Before my heart surgery, I held a loose grip on life. Because I knew that Kirby was already in Heaven, I would have been thrilled to join him. After surviving my heart surgery, I realized that I was still on earth for a reason. I began to heal from my losses. I had to face the fact that Kirby was never coming back. The physical pain of the heart surgery constantly reminded me of the emotional devastation caused by Kirby's absence.

I had to deliberately choose to connect with God and people and not to retreat into my own dark prison of grief. Having Mom and Dad stay with me was a huge blessing! Day and night, they ministered hope to me. My family and friends surrounded me with constant love and kindness. Sometimes I was able to pursue my grief recovery and sometimes others knew what to do for me. I was thrilled when Wendy would bring dinner and my grandboys. More than one person called and said, "Let's go for a walk" or "I want to take you to lunch." Staying connected with God and people who cared deeply about me gradually released me from the grip of grief.

By sharing this story with you, I received an even deeper level of healing. If you choose to share your story with others, you too can experience a greater level of freedom from grief.

Discussion Questions

1. If you haven't already, consider with whom can you share your grief story.

_____

_____

_____

_____

_____

_____

_____

2. As we journey through our grief, we may discover mindsets and thinking patterns that are not helpful. As we apply God's Word to these areas, we will experience growth and freedom. What are some of these areas in your life?

_____

_____

_____

_____

_____

_____

_____

_____

_____

_____

_____

_____

3. If you were free in these areas, how would your life be different? What would it look like?

_____

_____

_____

_____

_____

_____

_____

_____

_____

4. As widows, we may need help from others to be set free. In what ways do you see yourself needing others in the process of becoming free? Who do you think you can ask for help in these areas?

_____

_____

_____

_____

_____

_____

_____

_____

_____

_____

_____

_____

_____

_____

_____

Growing Stronger Guideline #4

THROW OFF EVERYTHING THAT HINDERS

With God's help, get rid of It!

CHAPTER FOUR

THROW OFF EVERYTHING THAT HINDERS
WITH GOD'S HELP, GET RID OF IT!

"Therefore, since we are surrounded by such a great cloud of witnesses, let us throw off everything that hinders and the sin that so easily entangles, and let us run with perseverance the race marked out for us" (Hebrews 12:1).

Some of us were blessed with a loving husband and are free from significant regrets. Thank God for this blessing. We may have enjoyed a wonderful marriage with a partner who loved us dearly and cheered us on in life. Our husbands who died in Christ have now joined that great cloud of witnesses, but we still have a race to run. Even so, if we want to run strong and last long in this race called the Christian life, we must free ourselves from things that hold us back.

What's Holding You Back?

The first step toward freedom from hindrances involves a decision on our part. We must ask, "Am I willing to let go of those things which have hindered me?" Until we respond with a resounding, "Yes!" we remain encumbered. These burdens don't just fall off. We must actively cast away anything that impedes our race. Then others can follow our example and throw off the weights that hold them back.

Do You Want to Be Free?

In John 5:1–15 (NKJV), we find the story of a man at the Pool of Bethesda. He suffered from a physical condition which had disabled him for 38 years. He was lying by the pool with a great number of people with various disabilities, waiting for a certain time when an angel went down into the pool and stirred the water. Whoever managed to step into the water first was healed of their disease.

Jesus came to the pool and saw this man lying there. Knowing that he had endured the infirmity a long time, Jesus asked him, "Do you want to be made well?" (v. 6).

What a strange question to ask a man who had been waiting so long to be healed!

The sick man replied, "Sir, I have no man to put me into the pool when the water is stirred up; but while I am coming, another steps down before me" (v. 7).

He did not realize that he was, at that very moment, speaking with the Son of God who had created him and all the angels! Jesus did not reveal Himself or scold this man for his helpless and hopeless attitude. He simply said, "Rise, take up your bed and walk." Immediately—after 38 long years—the man was healed, picked up his bed, and walked!

Now Jesus is challenging us through His Word, to throw off everything that hinders us! Like the man at the pool, we can choose how we will respond to Him. Initially, the man was focused on one solution—the angel stirring the water. Until that very moment, it was the only hope he had.

When the Son of God spoke to him, he couldn't see past his own "stuckness" to the miraculous possibilities right in front of him! He responded by reasoning, "It's always been this way." Jesus gave him an assignment which required not only faith, but obedient action. He believed, obeyed, and was healed!

Similarly, it's very possible for the things that bog us down and impede our grief to masquerade as old friends. We may not be fully aware of our need for change. Or perhaps we do recognize a need for change, but our misguided coping patterns have morphed into destructive habits. We want to be free but can too easily become accustomed to the familiarity of our baggage. To venture out into freedom requires risk, which can appear frightening. Or we try to change, fail, and, like the man at the pool, remain defeated, hopeless, and helpless.

Considering all these challenges, how do we deal with the tendency toward complacency? We must actively resist hanging onto our old baggage. If we want to be free, our first and most important decision requires both faith and action: THROW IT OFF!

With God's Help, Get Rid of It!

When we are ready to make that decision, how do we do it? White-knuckling it may work for a while, but deep and permanent change requires more than a decision plus will power. To change directions in life, we need clear guidance and lots of support. GriefShare and other widows' groups often provide important comfort, camaraderie, encouragement, and structure. In order to benefit from this support system, it is imperative to stay connected to God and other Christians. Isolation can be risky! Attend church. Join a Bible study. Be sure to surround yourself with those who understand the importance of living a life of godly choices and discarding destructive behaviors.

God has good plans for anyone who turns to Him. He promises in Psalm 51:17 that He will not despise anyone who comes to Him with a broken and contrite heart. But humility is only the first step. God doesn't stop there! If we give our lives over to God, it is He Himself who gives you "the desire and the power to do what pleases Him" (Philippians 2:13, NLT). As in the case of the man at the pool, Jesus empowers us to do what we previously could not do in our own strength. Not only does Jesus help us, but He gives us a ready-made support system in the Body of Christ, the Church.

Stay the Course.

More than recovery, God has GREAT dreams and plans for each of us in partnership with Him! Ephesians 2:10 says, "We are God's handiwork, created in Christ Jesus to do good works, which God prepared in advance for us to do." He wants us to soak up His Word, saturate ourselves in His aspirations, and then ask Him for big things! When we do this, we can be confident that His power will enable us because He has promised, "If you remain in me and my words remain in you, ask whatever you wish, and it will be done for you" (John 15:7).

At times like this, remember to keep focused on Jesus, "the Author and the Finisher of your faith" (Hebrews 12:2). He has begun the good work in you, and He completes what He starts! He will continue working in and through you until the day you cross the ultimate finish line in Heaven (Philippians 1:6).

Get Up, Again!

Sometimes widows are afraid to start a journey for fear that they will fail. Taking the first step may require putting the fear of failure to rest by realizing that it is actually true: humans will fail. That's why we need a Savior! Jesus is the only perfect human who ever walked this earth. But because He is also fully God, He is able to provide forgiveness and restore us when we are less than perfect! If we fall, we rise again, not by hiding in shame, but by approaching "God's throne of grace with confidence, so that we may receive mercy and find grace to help us in our time of need" (Hebrews 4:16)!

Discussion Questions

1. How would you describe the "race" you are running? Is it a "marathon" or a "sprint"? Why?

_____

_____

_____

_____

_____

_____

_____

_____

2. Ask God to show you how He sees your "race." Is there anything that is slowing you down from running the way you would like? What would be involved in "throwing off" that hindrance in your life?

_____

_____

_____

_____

_____

_____

_____

_____

_____

_____

_____

3. Remember that we do not run alone or in our own strength. Commit your "race" to God and ask Him to free you from anything that is slowing you down or causing you to stumble.

_____

_____

_____

_____

_____

_____

_____

_____

_____

Growing Stronger Guideline #5

KEEP LOOKING UP

Make *PERSONAL GROWTH* an even higher priority
than resolving your grief.

CHAPTER FIVE

KEEP LOOKING UP
FIX OUR EYES ON JESUS

"Let us fix our eyes on Jesus, the author and perfecter of our faith, who for the joy set before Him endured the cross, scorning its shame, and sat down at the right hand of the throne of God" (Hebrews 12:2).

Is it possible that many so-called "coincidences" are actually God secretly intervening in our lives in ways that we do not recognize? Keeping our eyes fixed on Jesus will help us realize that His hand is at work in our daily circumstances. As we are aware of God's presence, we are reminded of Psalm 139:5: "You have enclosed me behind and before and laid Your hand upon me" (NASB). In other words, He is hugging us with one arm and leading us with the other!

I (Dr. Meier) developed a four-point prayer which I pray almost every morning. You will find all four of these principles incorporated into our Twelve Growing Stronger Guidelines for overcoming and growing through grief.

Dr. Meier's Four-Point Morning Prayer:

1. **Lord, help me to become more like You today.** Because of this simple prayer, I am able to fix my eyes on Jesus. If anything goes wrong today, I can thank God, even in the middle of the problem, because I know it will help me accomplish the desire I prayed for that very morning—to become more like Jesus. Without hardships and disappointments, I will not grow very rapidly. I also pray that God will help me be a good listener and learn as much as possible the easy way!

2. **Lord, help me to serve You today.** My goal is not for personal gain, but for God to reach out, in love, through me today to "dance with the world" in some way that will bless at least one person.

3. **Lord, help me to stay out of trouble today.** I know I am a sinner, fully capable of sins of omission and commission. But all sin hurts somebody—God, others, or me—so I really do not want to yield to the temptation to sin.

4. **Lord, help me to learn and grow from whatever may go wrong today.** I expect to lead a normal life, and all normal lives include some setbacks, failures, and crises. I expect to suffer

one or more disappointments each day. When most days go by without one, I consider those bonus days!

If I am able to fix my eyes on Jesus, I will see things from an eternal perspective. I used to get angry, even with God, when I experienced disappointments and crises. I would be surprised, and even shocked by them, as though somehow, I was entitled to a calamity-free life. I also tended to "catastrophize"—to assume the worst scenario—when trouble did arise. Now I can step back a bit, gain perspective, and realize that God will help me through whatever comes my way. In fact, He will even use it to grow me up!

Focus, Focus...

This new kind of perspective emerges from repeatedly choosing to focus our eyes on Jesus. What a beautiful alternative to constantly paying attention to ourselves and our problems! It is only natural for humans to be somewhat self-absorbed. It is easy to turn our gaze inward and concentrate on our own needs and wants.

When the Bible uses the term "fix," it is not referring to a casual glance, but purposefully turning away from one thing to focus on something else. It is difficult to fix our eyes on our own problems and on Jesus at the same time. But deliberately pondering His insight on our predicaments is very practical, since obsessing about our struggles doesn't work anyway. Jesus has better solutions to our problems.

A Far-sighted Perspective

Sometimes ordeals loom so large that it is hard to think about anything else. When we lose our spouse, grief can be all-consuming. That's when we need faith and patience to help us turn our gaze away from our grief and toward Jesus, who can give us a new perspective. Keeping our eyes on Jesus can remind us that God is *for us*, not *against us*. His purposes are higher than ours.

A building at the center of Biola University, in La Mirada, California, displays a beautiful, thirty-foot-tall mural of Jesus. He is dressed in a red robe and holding out a large black Bible. Often referred to as "The Jesus Mural," this stunning work, gifted to the campus by talented muralist Kent Twitchell in 1990, is officially entitled, "The Word." In addition to its beauty, those who walk by are often amazed that, because of the mural's height, it appears that Jesus' gaze is always upon them.

We know, from Psalm 139, that God has been closely watching

over us, keenly interested in every aspect of our lives, from our very conception until this moment. Now, He is asking that we keep our eyes on Him! As we do, we will soon realize that no matter how big our problems may appear, Jesus is much, much BIGGER! And His eyes are always upon us!

From Crisis to Opportunity

While we can take comfort in Romans 8:28 (that God will work everything together for our good), Romans 8:29 is every bit as important as verse 28. In verse 29 we learn that Jesus "foreknew" that you would become a believer someday. Other passages in the Bible inform us that before God even created this world, He could look into the future and know you personally and intimately. Verse 29 continues that God's goal for your life is for you to become conformed to the image of Christ. This means that God wants you to develop deeper and deeper character and love, like the character and love of Jesus.

Think about that for a minute or two. *When you are grieving, God still loves you and feels empathy for you.* Jesus knows how you feel because He also suffered many trials during His earthly life. He wants to help you. But from His eternal perspective, His larger goal is to conform you to the image of Christ. He wants to help you solve your problems, but He will use what you learn from your grief as a tool in His hands to carve you into a beautiful woman of character.

But maximizing trials to conform you to the image of Jesus does not mean that God brought this trouble upon you. After He helps you overcome this present difficulty, He promises to make you stronger than ever!

The Bible says we can be thankful in all things, but it takes a real saint to be thankful during grief. Though it is often difficult, sometimes we succeed.

Freedom from Focusing on Our Fear

Fixing our eyes on Jesus can protect us from fears of loss and failure. Although we all suffer loss, we do not have to fear that it will destroy us.

The Bible tells of great widows such as Anna, Mary the mother of Jesus, Ruth and Naomi, and the widow of Zerephath, who endured immeasurable injury and sorrow. In all these cases, as they remained faithful to God, their distress eventually resulted in victory as God caused them to rise above it.

Distracted by "The Good"

Sometimes we simply get distracted from the Lord and fix our eyes on other things. Even good things, if deterring us from God's ways, become hindrances.

Luke 10:38–42 tells the story of two sisters who had the wonderful opportunity of hosting Jesus in their home. What an honor! As the story unfolds, we see that the sisters responded to the situation in two very different ways. While Martha extended the invitation and began all the preparations to serve Jesus, her sister Mary sat at Jesus' feet and heard His teaching.

Martha was a conscientious hostess but got a little carried away. She was so worried and anxious about working for Jesus that she forgot to take the time to enjoy Him, as Mary did. When Martha complained to Jesus about Mary not helping, instead of scolding Mary and sending her into the kitchen, Jesus tenderly called Martha by name—twice! He acknowledged that she was distracted about many things and taught her the one essential that brings everything else into focus: turning her attention to Jesus. He surprised Martha by encouraging her to become more like Mary.

"Only one thing is needed," Jesus said. "Mary has chosen what is better, and it will not be taken away from her" (vs. 42).

I (Mary Beth) have often contemplated the irony of my own name, as I have a strong tendency to be a "Martha" rather than a "Mary." I have been blessed with good endurance and a strong work ethic, but I regularly have to rein myself in from overworking. Like Mary, I absolutely LOVE to spend time "sitting at Jesus' feet," reading the Bible and praying in my gazebo. One of the greatest joys in my life has been meeting with dear friends for Bible study and prayer. Still, I have to be careful not to be bullied by the busyness of my to-do lists, or I am in danger of going into full-blown "Martha-mode." My family would tell you that we have much more peace and joy in our home if my heart maintains a "Mary posture" at the feet of Jesus, as I go about my daily work.

Stay Alert

Finally, in our efforts to focus on Jesus, we must remain aware of the fact that we have an enemy who would love to derail us. He is more than happy to throw temptation before us in the form of the cares of this world, the deceitfulness of riches, and the desire for other things (Mark 4:19).

Another role of the devil is to accuse Christians, especially when you have suffered loss. He will try to discourage you, shake your confidence, and even try to make you hate yourself. He tries to convince you to give up in times of crisis. He will attempt to distract or discourage you.

That's why 1 Peter 5:8 cautions us to, "Be self-controlled and alert. Your enemy the devil prowls around like a roaring lion looking for someone to devour."

Aside from outward influences, our own weak flesh can also lead us off track. The fatigue of grief and the necessary routines of daily life can cause us to lose focus. Fortunately, in Christ we have the protection from the enemy we need, and the power of the Holy Spirit to overcome the weaknesses of our flesh.

A United Focus

We can also take courage as we continually remind ourselves that we do not have to do this alone. The Scripture says, "Let US fix OUR eyes" (Hebrews 12:2, emphasis ours). As the Body of Christ, we are in this together as we look to Jesus: our Example, our Helper, our Teacher, our Source, our Comforter, our "Older Brother," our God, the Author and Perfecter of our faith!

Discussion Questions

1. The Lord's Prayer begins with, "Our Father, who art in Heaven, hallowed be Thy name" (Matthew 6:9). Jesus was teaching us to get our eyes on God and His character before we tell Him about our prayer needs. Take a few moments and list some of the ways we can "hallow His name"- bring praise and glory to His name.

_____

_____

_____

_____

_____

_____

_____

2. Read the account of Peter walking on the water in Matthew 14:22–33. What caused Peter to walk on the water? What caused Peter to be afraid? What happened when he was afraid? How does this apply to your grief journey?

_____

_____

_____

_____

_____

_____

_____

_____

3. Taking our eyes off Jesus and looking at the storm around us can cause us to falter in our faith. Focusing on Jesus strengthens our faith, as He is the Author and Perfecter of our faith! Consider what situations in your life have caused you to look at "the wind" instead of Jesus. Take a moment now to praise the Lord for His wonderful name, and then release those cares to Him.

_____

_____

_____

_____

_____

_____

_____

_____

_____

_____

_____

4. In what ways have you grown stronger than you ever were before as a result of working through grief?

_____

_____

_____

_____

_____

_____

_____

_____

_____

Growing Stronger Guideline #6

HANG IN THERE

Whenever you feel like giving up, endure.

CHAPTER SIX

HANG IN THERE

FOR THE JOY SET BEFORE YOU ... ENDURE!

"Let us fix our eyes on Jesus, the author and perfecter of our faith, who for the joy set before him endured the cross, scorning its shame, and sat down at the right hand of the throne of God" (Hebrews 12:2).

Hang in There!

Endurance!! The challenges of life can be really tough sometimes! Even Thomas Edison, an absolute genius and one of the greatest inventors of all time, declared, "Genius is one percent inspiration, and ninety-nine percent perspiration" *(Quotes.net, STANDS4 LLC, 2014. "Thomas Edison Quotes." n.d.)*. Although it was hard work, because Edison persevered through many failed inventions, we can now easily flip a switch and enjoy incandescent light—just one of his many inventions of great value. His dreams spurred him on to overcome obstacles.

Helen Keller is another courageous example of endurance. As a toddler, Helen's sight and hearing were destroyed by a mysterious and extremely high fever. She triumphed over deafness and blindness to become an author, speaker, and world-renowned humanitarian. Recognized by Winston Churchill as "the greatest woman of our age" *(Helen Keller Foundation n.d.)*, Helen was the first deaf and blind person to receive a Bachelor of Arts degree. She also received honorary doctorate degrees from six universities around the world, including Harvard, and met every American President from Grover Cleveland to Lyndon B. Johnson.

An inspiration to those of us who struggle with far less, Helen exhorted, "We differ, blind and seeing, one from another, not in our senses, but in the use we make of them, in the imagination and courage with which we seek wisdom beyond the senses." And again, "A happy life consists not in the absence, but in the mastery of hardships" *(Helen Keller Biography n.d.)*.

But behind this great woman was another great woman, Helen's teacher, Anne Sullivan, who also had overcome great adversity. Born into extreme poverty, Anne suffered the loss of many family members by death or desertion. At age five, her eyesight was severely damaged by a disease called Trachoma. Anne and her little brother Jimmy were sent to live at the poor house, where Jimmy died three months later *(Anne Sullivan Biography n.d.)*.

Alone and desperate for a better life, Anne escaped the poor house by going to Perkins School for the Blind. Not only did Anne learn braille and receive an education, but she later underwent surgery which restored much of her eyesight. Although Anne was quite ignorant, academically and socially when she began her schooling, she graduated as valedictorian of her class! In June 1886, she delivered a graduation speech where she challenged her fellow students, "Duty bids us go forth into active life. Let us go cheerfully, hopefully, and earnestly, and set ourselves to find our special part. When we have found it, willingly and faithfully perform it; for every obstacle we overcome, every success we achieve tends to bring man closer to God."

With this clear mission, Anne went on to become Helen Keller's teacher. She used the braille skills she had learned at Perkins to unlock the turbulent, dark, and silent world in which Helen lived. Because Anne had also been a troubled and difficult child afflicted with blindness, she was able to love Helen despite Helen's early tantrums and obstinacy. She didn't give up, and through faith, love, and perseverance, she found the jewel of a girl trapped inside Helen's little deaf and blind body. Without the challenges that Anne had overcome and her resulting sense of mission, she never would have reached Helen and equipped her to become one of the most inspirational women of all time.

First, Anne needed to teach Helen the very concept of language, and then she led her to explore the wonderful new life before her. Later, Helen described the moment she learned her first word, "water": "The mystery of language was revealed to me. I knew then that 'w-a-t-e-r' meant the wonderful cool something that was flowing over my hand. That living word awakened my soul, gave it light, hope, joy, set it free!" (Helen Keller Biography n.d.). Helen continues to describe the arduous learning process: "Gradually from naming an object we advance step by step until we have traversed the vast distance between our first stammered syllable and the sweep of thought in a line of Shakespeare."

Heroes, such as Edison, Keller, and Sullivan, can encourage and inspire us to carry on when life gets tough. But only one "Hero," Jesus, will be ever-present when difficulties may cause us to feel as though we can't go on. At these points, it is critical that we consider His example as the Author and Perfecter of our faith. As the Author of our faith, Christ has given us new life. As the Perfecter of our faith, He won't give up on us in hard times but will use those difficult periods to continue to refine us, *not define us!*

How Did Jesus Do It?

As we "fix our eyes" on Jesus, we see the perfect example of endurance. How did Jesus do it? First of all, He endured the cross. Yes, Jesus was fully God, but amazingly, He was fully human as well. His physical body felt every lash of the whip, every nail, every excruciating breath. More than 700 years before the birth of Jesus, the Prophet Isaiah described Jesus' appearance as so disfigured that it was "beyond that of any man and His form marred beyond human likeness" (Isaiah 52:14), yet He endured it!

Jesus endured the cross. But why did He do this? And how was it possible? Hebrews 12:2 says that the "joy set before Him" helped Him to endure. Jesus did not suffer for nothing! What was the "joy" that helped Him endure such torment? In short, WE are His joy. WE are His reward for suffering!

When we are suffering through grief, depression leads us to the misbelief that there is no way out—no light at the end of the tunnel. But as therapists, every day, Dr. Meier and Mary Beth experience those who have endured and found the joy at the end of their tunnel of pain. We, too, must have faith that there is "joy set before us" and endure until we get there. As Mary Beth's late husband Bob often said, "One day, this pain will fade and will seem like a distant memory. Then there will be joy again."

Jesus had to be willing to live in a flesh-and-blood body in order to be like us. But because He was also fully God, when He suffered death, He accomplished several amazing things. First of all, He tasted death for everyone. He experienced everything that we suffer as humans, even every type of temptation to fail or give up.

He paid the price to bring all those who will believe in Him to Heaven. He took the sins of the world upon Himself and died for all, so that we could live eternally. He blazed the way for each of us to become children of God.

I (Mary Beth) watched my dear husband Bob suffer valiantly, briefly, and intensely, with cancer for three months. Bob's faith in God never wavered. Though he fought courageously, Bob's pain ended on June 13, 2019, when Jesus Himself carried Bob to Heaven. I was comforted, during Bob's illness, to recall that Jesus had suffered —far more than Bob ever did—when He died on the cross to take away our sins and prepare the way for us to join Him in Heaven someday. In this great truth, our family stood firmly at Bob's side.

Jesus' death and resurrection sealed His victory over our enemy.

Satan's death sentence has already been signed and will, in God's time, be executed.

Jesus has also freed us from the fear of death! I (Linda) used to be afraid of death, but I saw my husband Kirby leave this earth and go to Heaven. That is the worst pain a person can suffer. The man with whom I was one went away. The trauma I suffered is 100 points on the Holmes and Rahe stress scale. There is no greater loss. After surviving the initial grief, it came to me that I could probably endure anything. I had lost my fear of death. What could anyone do to me that I could not endure? As widows, we know that the end of this life is only the beginning of eternal life with Christ. So, what's the big deal?

It's Easier to Endure When You Understand "The Why"

What if Jesus had not endured? What if He had not paid the purchase price for us? How many times have we decided to quit when faced with much lesser challenges? Jesus knew exactly why the Father had sent Him into the world. "For God did not send His Son into the world to condemn the world, but that the world through Him might be saved" (John 3:17, NKJV). Thank God Jesus didn't give up halfway to the cross! He is our example to never quit!

After the loss of her husband, a widow may be tempted to give up because the pain of grief is excruciating. Again, we are reminded that Jesus' pain was even worse than that of the widow. In fact, according to the New Oxford American Dictionary, the word "excruciating" comes from the 16th century Latin verb, "excruciat" meaning "tormented," based on the word "crux," or "a cross." Yet even while suffering on the cross, Isaiah 53:4 says that Jesus also bore OUR griefs and carried away OUR sorrows—including the unspeakable anguish of losing our husbands.

Jesus Understands When Enduring Gets Hard

Jesus understands suffering. He knows that life in this fallen world includes seasons of loss and grief. Yet, He encourages us to "be of good cheer," because He has overcome the world (John 16:33)!

But how can we "be of good cheer" when we feel defeated and depressed? When things seem hopeless? When we are depressed, a chemical called "serotonin" gets depleted in the brain, influencing us to think that we will never get better. The severe trauma of losing a spouse can also deplete serotonin in the brain, resulting in depression and anxiety. But, we widows can overcome depression with the right kind of guidance and assistance. Sometimes this may include medication for those who may have inherited low serotonin production. Taking medication for depression and anxiety during grief is just as reasonable as taking insulin for diabetes. A chemical imbalance in our bodies needs to be treated.

There is No Shame in Showing our Emotions

Some of us grew up in homes where we felt guilty if we expressed distressing emotions. Rather than receiving comfort from the adults in our lives, we were shamed, criticized, and even ridiculed for crying. We were taught that crying showed weakness. We believed the lies of the authority figures in our lives.

Pastoral Counselor Rev. Chris Taylor of *Candlelight Ministries* suggests processing our grief this way:

1. Don't shove the feelings down.
2. Allow the pain of that grief to come up from your toes, all the way up through your head.
3. Let it out through tears from your eyes or vocal expressions from your mouth, such as words, groanings and shouts. Get it out!

When we suffer great loss, our pain will seek expression. Crying is appropriate—even healthy and necessary—to process our grief. Missionary Ruth Ost Martinez, of Calvary Ministerial Institute, in Mexico, lost her husband and partner in ministry Victor in September of 2019. Though a new widow herself, Ruth has ministered to many new widows. When Ruth becomes aware of a new widow, she drives her up into the mountains. On the way, Ruth talks to the new widow about the Holy Spirit and her husband. She then asks if she can sing to her. As she sings the widow's emotions begin to rise within her. She begins to cry and then finally expresses the deep, deep sobs that have been trapped inside her. Sometimes Ruth gets out of the car or lets the widow out of the car so she can shout, scream, and wail. Other times, Ruth will simply hold the widow while she sobs.

Ruth shared how her husband Victor Martinez would always walk next to her with his hand on her shoulder. Ruth said that she loved sensing Victor's hand on her shoulder as she always felt very loved and secure. Through Victor's subtle touch, Ruth experienced his protection, direction and sometimes even his gentle correction!

In Spanish, the Holy Spirit is the "Consolador"—one who is at your side. Ruth reminds herself and other widows that the Holy Spirit is always at your side. He says, "I'm here for you. You are not alone. I will be at your side."

At times, Victor and Ruth recorded teachings for television. The

Director of Production would give them earbuds. He would instruct them not to listen to other voices, but only the voice of the Director through their earbuds. In a similar way, Ruth encourages new widows that this is an opportunity to get to know the Holy Spirit in a new way. Like the Director, He will whisper guidance in your ear. Says Ruth, "He's my Counselor. He's my Director of Production. He will help, guide, comfort and convict me."

Further, Ruth encourages new widows to read Psalm 139 and pray each verse back to God. Since Psalm 139 speaks of God's intimate knowledge of and care for each individual, this is especially comforting to women who are relearning who they are—in God's eyes—as a single person.

Finally, Ruth encourages widows to reach out to comfort other widows. In the process of comforting others, we, too, experience God's comfort.

Jesus empathizes with us. As the Prophet Isaiah described, "He was despised and rejected—a man of sorrows, acquainted with deepest grief. We turned our backs on Him and looked the other way. He was despised, and we did not care" (Isaiah 53:4, NLT). He faced a mock trial, was publicly humiliated, betrayed, falsely accused, abandoned by friends, slandered, and taunted, but His response to all this was to *shame the shame!* Jesus knew who He was and why He came to earth. He did not allow Himself to be defined by what others did to Him or said about Him.

Emotions are not sinful. God gave them to us, and Jesus experienced them all! When I (Mary Beth) lost Bob, I didn't even know that such emotional pain existed. This profound anguish was greater than my intense joy at giving birth. I was comforted to know that no matter how much I suffered, Jesus knew, and Jesus understood because He suffered more than I ever possibly could. Jesus understands and has compassion for my distressing emotions.

There are Rewards Ahead!

After Jesus endured the pain and scorned the shame, He received the acclaim of His Father in Heaven. As we endure hardship, we can expect that God will also bring good out of our situations. As an unknown author has said, "Everything will be okay in the end. If it's not okay, it's not the end!"

When we lose our husbands, some may question, "Does God still love me?" When we face adversity, it is natural to wonder whether we are in God's will. Romans 8:39 says that His primary will is for us to become more like Jesus, "conformed to the image of Christ." God still wants us to be our own unique selves, but to become better equipped to love and be loved, just like Jesus loves and is loved.

When adversity tries to intimidate us, we can follow Christ's example and endure—and even rejoice—while looking by faith to a better future. We can "consider it all joy" (James 1:2–4), knowing that this testing time will eventually result in greater endurance and maturity. We will grow through our pain and come out whole at the other end. Our faith, though tested by fire, will shine like gold which will bring glory and honor to God. So, when you suffer:

DO NOT:
- Be ashamed to express your emotions
- Grow weary and lose heart

DO:
- Keep Christ in focus and heavenly rewards in mind
- Endure the pain
- Scorn the shame
- Receive the acclaim of our Father in Heaven

Then He will say, "Well done, good and faithful servant! You have been faithful with a few things; I will put you in charge of many things. Come and share your master's happiness!" (Matthew 25:21).

Discussion Questions

1. The opposite of enduring is quitting! What is at stake if you quit? What do you stand to gain if you endure?

_____

_____

_____

_____

_____

_____

_____

_____

_____

2. We have an enemy whose methods are to steal, kill, and destroy; including his efforts to keep us from fulfilling the destiny (the race marked out for us) that God has in store. The Apostle Paul taught us in 2 Corinthians 2:11 that we must be aware of his schemes so that he will not outwit us. What are some things against which you can be on your guard so that the enemy does not succeed in his efforts to make you give up the race? How can you strengthen yourself in these areas?

_____

_____

_____

_____

_____

_____

_____

_____

_____

3. The Apostle Peter taught us in 1 Peter 5:8–9 to be self-controlled and alert against the enemy's tactics, resisting him while standing firm in the faith, knowing that other Christians throughout the world are experiencing similar sufferings. Fellowship with other widows helps us stand strong. With whom can you fellowship to help you stand strong and endure?

_____

_____

_____

_____

_____

_____

_____

_____

_____

Growing Stronger Guideline #7
DON'T LOSE HEART!

When you experience discipline, remind yourself that God is a good Father and say, "My Abba (Daddy) Father loves me."

CHAPTER SEVEN
DON'T LOSE HEART
ACCEPT THE LORD'S TRAINING

*"No discipline is enjoyable while it is happening—it's painful!
But afterward, there will be a peaceful harvest of right living
for those who are trained in this way" (Hebrews 12:11).*

In the Bible, we read an entire book about the experiences of Job, who was a moral, loving and innocent man, but who nevertheless suffered a severe crisis involving a horrible and painful skin disease, and eventually the death of his own children. His wife and friends gave him what God Himself called bad advice, telling him his troubles must be due to sins Job had committed. Likewise, well-meaning people may give you all kinds of bad counsel when your husband passes away. God may have allowed your husband to die for a variety of reasons that none of us will completely understand until we get to Heaven and ask Him. When Job's wife was attempting to lay a guilt trip on him, Job correctly and wisely replied, "What? Shall we expect good from God and not also expect adversity?" (Job 2:10) Whatever we suffer, we can be assured that God ultimately wants good things for our lives. So, in your crisis, search to find what God wants to teach you now, but don't let people lay a guilt trip on you.

God is a Good Father!

We are God's precious daughters. Though He must discipline us at times, He is not an abusive father, but a loving heavenly Father, who teaches and corrects us, when necessary. We can be sure that God's discipline is helping us to look more like His Son, our Big Brother Jesus.

As good parents, we would not consider neglecting the training of our children. Sometimes, especially with a strong-willed child, it can be a very difficult task. We persist, however, for we want our children to obey us for their own good. We want our children to respect us and learn to live godly lives. If we, as parents, want our children to respect us, "how much more should we submit to the Father of our spirits and live?" (Hebrews 12:9)

Sometimes, even in little things, God also corrects us, for our own good and to bless others. It may not always make sense to us, but God has His reasons. Recently, I (Mary Beth) had such an opportunity to experience my Father's gentle course correction.

One morning, I had so much to do that I prayed for peace and asked God, "Please, order my steps." I knew my tendency to worry, like Martha, about so many things to do, but in my heart, I wanted to be like Mary and at least "sit at Jesus' feet" as I went about my work. With my to-do list before me, I repeated Proverbs 16:3 to the Lord as I prayed about the day ahead, "Commit your actions to the LORD, and your plans will succeed" (NLT). "Thank you, Lord, that You care about what concerns me today," I prayed.

I also knew that sometimes I could run ahead of God with my own plans, so I prayed, "Help me, Lord, not to be rebellious if You direct me a way that I don't really want to go. I know that Your ways are best. Please, go before me and even help me to obey You."

I needed to stop at a department store, and also pick up a few things at the hardware store. I headed to the hardware store but felt a nudge in my heart to go to the department store first.

"Hmm, that's funny," I thought. "I wonder why the Lord would care which store I go to first..." But since I had prayed, I followed that "still, small voice" and headed to the department store.

I collected the items on my list and then felt an urgency to pay and get going. Again, I thought that was curious, but I have walked with the Lord long enough to know that He always has His reasons, which are better than mine. Although I admit that I did look for one last thing to put in my cart, I paid and hurried to the car.

Because I had gone to the department store first, the shortest way to the hardware store was through the grocery store parking lot. As I pulled into the lot, a young man, with his pants sagging, jumped out of his friend's car and ran into the store. His wallet fell out of his pants right in front of my car!

I hopped out of my car, grabbed the wallet, parked, and chased him down near the back of the store!

He was shocked, not even knowing that he had lost his wallet! He threw his arms around my neck and said, "Thank God! Thank you!" and "God bless you!" over and over!

"Not many people would do that!" he exclaimed.

"Well, I'm a Christian, too!" I replied.

"Yes, Ma'am!" he said, just glowing.

I winked and told him that losing his wallet was a consequence of sagging pants.

"Yes, Ma'am," he said. "I'll pull them up right now!" And he did!

Later we saw each other in the parking lot, and he excitedly told his friend, "That's her!"

He waved and called out to me, "God bless you again!"

I told him of my morning prayer and we just praised God together! Praise the Lord for His goodness and the joy of walking with Him!

It's for My Own Good? Really?

Yes, really!

We may respond to discipline in several ways:

1. We can accept it with resignation.
2. We can accept it with self-pity, thinking we really don't deserve it.
3. We can be angry and resentful toward God.
4. We can accept it gratefully, as the appropriate response we owe a loving Father (Life Application Study Bible, NLT, p. 2108).

If we choose to accept what God is teaching us in the middle of our grief, Hebrews 12:11 says that "it produces a harvest of righteousness and peace for those who have been trained by it." If we can endure the discomfort of the training process, we will reach our goal of godliness. It will be worth it!

So, what will be your response?

Missionaries to Mexico, Victor and Ruth Martinez, have ministered to thousands of people in over 40 countries. After Victor died, Ruth reached out to many new widows in Mexico with her personal, 5-point Grief Survival Strategy:

1. Cry. You need to! This is how you get the grief out.
2. Forgive, forgive, forgive. Forgive yourself. Forgive the doctor. Forgive the drunk driver or the assassin.
3. Say, "Thank you" to God. Recognize that only God gives and takes life. Thank God that He took your husband to Heaven. Thank Him that you are a widow.
4. Start every day by finding three things for which to be thankful.
5. Each day, find a worship song and sing it all day long to prevent yourself from sliding into "the dumps."

Ruth admitted that it was exceedingly difficult to arrive at the point of being thankful to God for taking Victor to Heaven and that she was now a widow. She continued to express her thanks, and she began to believe it. Then she felt such relief!

Let's refer back to Job. How did he respond to his pain? Job's tremendous loss was not a disciplinary action from God; however, he did learn a lot through his crisis. Sometimes Job was so overwhelmed with grief that all he could do was to sit silently. At other times, Job talked to God and God talked to him. Though Job poured out his heart to God, the Bible says that "In all this, Job did not sin in what he said" (Job 2:10). In fact, later, reflecting on his trials, Job declared to his misguided, well-meaning friends, "But He knows the way that I take; when He has tested me, I will come forth as gold" (Job 23:10).

In the end, Job did not lose heart as he trusted God through devastating circumstances. He learned that God is God and that he was God's creation. He understood that in a fallen world, bad things sometimes happen to good people. Similarly, after the loss of our husbands, we can still trust that God is working for our good as He leads and guides us through our grief.

Discussion Questions

1. Times of suffering can also be times of new growth. In what ways do you feel the Lord is helping you to grow?

_____

_____

_____

_____

_____

_____

_____

_____

_____

_____

_____

_____

2. Looking back on your life, what are some lessons that you have learned from your loving heavenly Father? What are some benefits that you see in your life now that are the results from painful circumstances in the past?

_____

_____

_____

_____

_____

_____

_____

_____

3. Have you ever had friends like Job's who gave you bad advice, falsely blaming you for the crisis? How did you handle it?

_____

_____

_____

_____

_____

_____

_____

_____

Growing Stronger Guideline #8
DON'T GROW WEARY

Remember that your victory is just around the corner.

CHAPTER EIGHT
DON'T GROW WEARY
STRENGTHEN YOURSELF FOR THE RACE

"Therefore, strengthen your feeble arms and weak knees.
Make level paths for your feet, so that the lame may
not be disabled, but rather healed" (Hebrews 12:12–13).

Training for the Race of Life

The Apostle Paul often compares this Christian life to a race. The starting line is the day we accept Jesus into our hearts. The finish line is when we complete this earthly race, receive the prize for which God has called us, and meet Jesus face to face. The unique thing about this race, though, is that we run the race and train at the same time! There are no "practice runs!" Paul cheers us on in Philippians 3:14, where he describes his own race: "I press on toward the goal to win the prize for which God has called me heavenward in Christ Jesus." In the meantime, as Hebrews 12:12 says, we are to "strengthen our feeble arms and weak knees."

My (Mary Beth's) daughter, Christa, is a long-distance runner. Bob and I enjoyed watching her run as we cheered her on through many races during her high school and college years. Christa trained hard for her races. She was dedicated to her running schedule, diet, and rest. She explained that training not only maximized performance, but helped to prevent injury as well. She was careful to pay attention to her form so she would not get injured. Not only did Christa run hard, she ran smart!

A Marathon, Not a Sprint

The widow's life can be full of challenges—more of an arduous, cross-country marathon than a sprint on a well-manicured track! There are different types of races. Life is a marathon. But God's Word coaches us to train for whatever our particular race demands, as 1 Corinthians 9:26 (NLT) says, "So I run with purpose in every step."

In order to endure her marathon, the widow will need to practice good self-care. The death of her husband will disorganize her entire life. Sufficient rest, nutrition, exercise, time with the Lord, meaningful social connections, and recreation will eventually help her to regain her balance. These are things that no one else can do for her. It is her choice.

Some activities, like recreation and exercise can be done with others. Linda Smith, for example, has been walking regularly with her friend, Diane, for over 27 years. She still looks forward to it every time. Her husband Kirby affectionately referred to these outings as "Walkie-Talkies." After Kirby died, this familiar combination of exercise and socialization helped Linda connect with her next chapter in life.

Pace Yourself

In cross country, Christa described something called "finding your race pace"—that is, during training, finding the kind of pace you'd expect from yourself in order to complete a race. A common error for new runners is to run so fast in the first leg of the race that they are unable to sustain the pace, and they get passed up by other runners in the end.

Grief is exhausting. We also must learn to pace ourselves so that we can avoid burnout and finish strong in the race of life. This is difficult for some hard-driving personalities to accept, but if God rested one day during Creation, perhaps we can learn from His example and be patient with ourselves when we need to rest. If we don't, we may eventually disqualify ourselves from the race. Christa sadly told of one very athletic teammate who suffered a stress fracture in her foot, apparently from overuse. After that, she was not expected to be able to run competitively again. We need to pace ourselves so we can stay in the race!

While the Old Testament Jews practiced a strict weekly Sabbath, Hebrews 4 tells us that there is a rest for the people of God who "rest" in the finished work of Jesus Christ on the cross. Verse 11 tells us to "labor" to enter into that rest! So, ironically, our real work is to find our rest in Jesus' finished work, not our own!

Run with Courage

One decision a new widow will encounter is whether to continue running her race. At times, running seems like too much work. It takes courage to stay in the race, especially when she feels too tired to even get out of bed. While it is normal to be fatigued and require more sleep in the early days of widowhood, this typically resolves over time. If the fatigue persists or worsens, a visit to her doctor will help her rule out physical causes.

If a widow is past her ability to cope, she may begin to express thoughts such as, "I just can't do this" or "I just can't take this anymore." God understands the vulnerability of widows in such difficulty. He calls for the Body of Christ, beginning with the widow's family, to come to her aid. As James 1:27 (NLT) states, "Pure and genuine religion in the sight of God the Father, means caring for orphans and widows in their distress." As loved ones step up to assist the new widow—doing things for her that she cannot do for herself—she will be relieved of excess stress and can eventually return to better coping skills.

It's normal for a new widow to think about Heaven and even long to be there with her husband. This can become problematic, however, if these thoughts persist. Such statements as, "I wish I could just go to sleep and never wake up" or even, "I wish that Jesus would just come back today" are signs of what is known as passive suicidal ideation. When we feel overwhelmed, it's good to remember that God actually wants us to cast our cares on Him, not the other way around!

If a widow becomes so despondent that she is actively suicidal (i.e., she states an intent or plan to hurt herself), she needs professional help immediately. This is a psychiatric emergency. Call 9-1-1. It's important for family and friends to stay connected with the widow so they can monitor changes in behavior.

Suicide is **not** the way out! God promises hope! As 1 Cor. 10:13 reassures us, "No temptation has overtaken you except what is common to mankind. And God is faithful; He will not let you be tempted beyond what you can bear. But when you are tempted, He will also provide a way out so that you can endure it."

With the proper support of faith, family, friends, counseling, and medical care, widows can recover and return to the race.

Where are we going, anyway?

God's Word sets the course for our race. From before God formed us in the womb (Jeremiah 1:5), until we complete our race and spend eternity with Him, His "Word is a lamp unto our feet and a light unto our path" (Psalm 119:105).

When I (Mary Beth) was newly widowed, I was so devasted by the loss of my husband Bob that I was not able to concentrate long enough to read my Bible. I was also very distressed that the deep pain of grief prevented me from sensing God's presence the way I had since I became a Christian when I was a young girl. During this time, my dear friend read Christian books to me, then hugged and prayed with me. This was so meaningful, not only because I couldn't concentrate, but because Bob and I had previously enjoyed reading and praying together. Also, she was not afraid to hug me while I cried, which was a great comfort.

In every one of Christa's cross-country races, officials arrived early and marked out the course. Runners were led through a pre-race walk-through, so they knew the route. They learned where the course wound and where the hills and obstacles were. Not only did this help them stay on course, but they learned where the finish line was! Runners were able to envision the finish line while pacing themselves to complete the course.

Similarly, as officials mark out the course so that there are no surprises for the runners, we can minimize the ambushes of grief by planning ahead. Widows can anticipate special occasions such as birthdays, anniversaries, and holidays, and make arrangements to appropriately observe the day. This will offer her a greater sense of control over her emotions.

While we may be surprised by the twists and turns of our life's course, the Word of God tells us that our Finish Line is Heaven. Our husbands who lived for Jesus have preceded us to their own Finish Line. Those of us who are left behind must follow God as we walk by faith and not by sight on our way to our Finish Line (2 Corinthians 5:7).

Follow God—Don't Be Disqualified

If Heaven is our Finish Line, how do we get from here to there? In order to win this race, we must stay on course. Ephesians 5:1 says to "Follow God's example, therefore, as dearly loved children." While others may think they know a better way to go, Jesus said there is only one way to our Heavenly destination, and that is through Him. The road of grief may be difficult, and at times, running from our grief may appear to be an easier route. But Jesus tells us, "Enter through the narrow gate. For wide is the gate and broad is the road that leads to destruction and many enter through it. But small is the gate and narrow the road that leads to life, and only a few find it" (Matthew 7:13–14). Jesus is the Gate and Jesus is the only Way!

A good coach will work with his or her team to make sure that they know the rules of the race. The Bible tells us the rules for our race. Training may seem strict, but it's all in the runner's best interest. God's goal is to help us become the best spiritual athletes we can be—and not be disqualified along the way! We dare not allow ourselves to indulge in distractions by wasting our time or talents.

Even though our husbands have already crossed their Finish Lines, we who are left behind still have a race to complete. We are still here for a reason. We still have a calling on our lives. God still has work for us to do before we reach the Finish Line.

Christa said that when running the mile race, the third lap is always the hardest. After two laps around, generally the runner begins to feel tired. It is precisely when the runner is most tired that she needs to surge, making a special effort to run the third lap faster than the first two. She does this because she knows that in the fourth and final lap, the inspiration of being able to see the finish line will allow her to draw from inner resources and sprint the last leg of the race. As widows, we sometimes get tired. But this may be our third or fourth lap, and we need to pick up the pace! We want to run this race well! We want to hear Jesus say, "Well done, My good and faithful servant!" (Matthew 25:21)

Cross the Finish Line!

At the end of her race, it is critical for the runner to *think past* the finish line. If she is only running *to* it, she will start slowing down when she nears it. Quite the opposite, when one runs past the finish line, she will even throw out her chest and lean into the tape with all her might. Many a photo finish race has been won by these few inches!

Scotland's all-time greatest runner, Eric Liddell, knew what it meant to run in order to win the prize. When being interviewed about his fantastic pace in the 400-meter race he said, "The secret of my success over the 400 meters is that I run the first 200 meters as hard as I can. Then for the second 200 meters, with God's help, I run harder" *(Liddell n.d.).*

In life's great race, we never know when it's the last lap. So, let's keep running with all our might and all the strength that God gives us. Let's not grow weary and give up, but instead, look past the Finish Line to the prize God has for us!

Discussion Questions

1. Describe the things that have helped you most along your grief journey.

   _____

   _____

   _____

   _____

   _____

   _____

   _____

   _____

2. What are you adding or eliminating from your lifestyle to better your race?

   _____

   _____

   _____

   _____

   _____

   _____

   _____

   _____

   _____

   _____

   _____

   _____

   _____

   _____

3. It can be very encouraging to train with other people. Who would you consider to be on "your team" in this race? In what ways do you support each other?

_____

_____

_____

_____

_____

_____

_____

4. If you could not answer the above question to your satisfaction, consider the importance of developing "teammates." Bible studies, prayer groups, and support groups are a few ways to develop a support system which is so crucial to a grieving widow. What are some resources you could access to develop your support system?

_____

_____

_____

_____

_____

_____

_____

Growing Stronger Guideline #9

REMEMBER THAT GOD IS ON YOUR SIDE

God's love is not based on your performance,
but on His goodness.

CHAPTER NINE

REMEMBER THAT GOD IS ON YOUR SIDE
THE LORD IS FOR YOU!

*"The Spirit of the Lord is on me...to proclaim the year
of the Lord's favor and the day of vengeance of our God"
(Isaiah 61:2).*

How Much Does God Love Me?

In his book, *God Thinks You're Wonderful*, Max Lucado says, "God is fond of you. If He had a wallet, your photo would be in it. If God had a refrigerator, your picture would be on it. He sends you flowers every spring and a sunrise every morning... Face it, friend. He is crazy about you!"

Well, God did write a Book! And in His Book, He tells how much He loves you. Yes, YOU! "For God so loved the world that He gave His one and only Son, that whoever believes in Him shall not perish but have eternal life" (John 3:16).

God is Paying Attention to You

Does this sound too good to be true? If you ever doubt it, meditate on Psalm 139. You were fearfully and wonderfully made! When you fell asleep last night, God was thinking about you specifically. When you woke up this morning, He was thinking about you again. The number of times God thinks about you each day is so vast that you can't even count them! With one arm He hugs you and with the other He leads you. He is FOR you! He is there whether it feels that way or not.

But I Can't Feel Him

Sometimes the effects of grief can keep you from "feeling" the presence of God until you work through those memories. Often professional help is needed to do this. The truth is that while we live in this sinful world, whether we feel Him there or not, God is still there! And God is still good! He blesses us daily, sending the rain on the righteous and the unrighteous (Matthew 5:45).

If you struggle with sensing God's love because you can't feel his presence, consider what He sacrificed to express his great love for his children. We didn't deserve His love, but He loves us because He IS love. "Now, most people would not be willing to die for an upright person, though someone might perhaps be willing to die for a person who is especially good. But God showed His great love for us by sending Christ to die for us while we were still sinners" (Romans 5:7-8).

While this is, obviously, the ultimate love sacrifice, consider another way that Jesus loves us. In John 13:1 we read that, "Jesus knew that the hour had come for him to leave this world and go to the Father. Having loved his own who were in the world, He loved them to the end." Jesus then "got up from the table, took off His robe, wrapped a towel around His waist, and poured water into a basin. Then He began to wash the disciples' feet" (John 13:4-5). The King of the Universe stooped low to serve those He loved and asked us to follow His example as we love others.

I (Mary Beth) have experienced having someone else wash my feet. When Bob and I were dating, he surprised me at my door, holding a single white rose. He then asked if I would please bring him a basin of water, a towel, and some soap. Silently, Bob led me to sit on the couch while he knelt and washed my feet.

Amazed and overwhelmed by Bob's humble and loving devotion, I sobbed and sobbed as he gently washed and dried my feet. I was deeply touched by Bob's devotion and humility to God and to me. He promised that he would love me by humbly serving me. And he did. Later, Bob remarked that there was more water rolling down my cheeks than there was in the basin.

When he finished, Bob looked up and asked, "Mary Beth, will you marry me?"

Taken by surprise and flooded with emotion, I couldn't think for a moment! "I don't know!" I exclaimed.

"Well...will you be engaged to me?" Bob asked.

"Yes!" I agreed enthusiastically. "I'll be engaged to you!"

After many years of marriage, Bob sometimes teased that I was still trying to make up my mind. In reality, I decided right away! After nearly 39 years of lovingly serving our four children and me, Bob went to Heaven. This memory of his beautiful proposal, which revealed his gorgeous soul, is still my precious treasure.

In Luke 7:36-39, 44-50, we read about another foot washing. One of the Pharisees asked Jesus to have dinner with him, so Jesus went to his home and sat down to eat. When a certain immoral woman from that city heard He was eating there, she brought a beautiful alabaster jar filled with expensive perfume. Then she knelt behind Him at His feet, weeping. Her tears fell on His feet and she wiped them off with her hair. Then she kept kissing His feet and putting perfume on them.

When the Pharisee who invited Him saw this, he said to himself, "If this man were a prophet, He would know who is touching Him and what kind of woman is touching Him—that she is a sinner."

Jesus' response was:

Do you see this woman? I came into your house. You did not give me any water for my feet, but she wet my feet with her tears and wiped them with her hair. You did not give me a kiss, but this woman, from the time I entered, has not stopped kissing my feet. You did not put oil on my head, but she has poured perfume on my feet. Therefore, I tell you, her many sins have been forgiven—as her great love has shown. But whoever has been forgiven little loves little. Then Jesus said to her, 'Your sins are forgiven.'

Only a woman could have expressed her love for Jesus in this sweet way. Widows have a unique place in God's heart. Jesus paid special attention to widows. If you need to experience the love of God more deeply, envision Jesus washing your feet. As one of His disciples, you may also want to envision yourself washing His feet in response to His great love for you. As you worship Him, He will fill you with a sense of His loving presence.

In the Good Times/In the Bad Times

The problem of pain in this world causes many of us to think, "So, if God is for me, He loves me, and He is thinking about me night and day, then why does He allow bad things in my life?" or "Why did He allow my husband to die?" Whether your husband died quickly or suffered for a season, you may question how a loving God would allow his passing. The truth is that God's love does not exempt you from trials, but in the midst of them you can be assured that God is for you. Romans 8:31 says, "What, then, shall we say in response to this? If God is for us, who can be against us?" "These very trials, though painful at the time, can strengthen our faith so that we develop perseverance and become mature, not lacking in anything" (James 1:3–4).

There are times, however, when, due to the fallen condition of this world, we suffer at the hands of other people. A negligent doctor or nurse, a careless or drunk driver, or an irresponsible caregiver may have been at fault for our husband's death.

At other times, an outright evil person may have caused the death of our husband. Psalm 18: 6, 13, tells us that God is enraged at this! "In my distress I cried out to the Lord; yes, I prayed to my God for help. He heard me from His sanctuary. My cry to Him reached His ears." "The Lord thundered from Heaven. The voice of the Most High resounded amid the hail and burning coals." God was mad about evil things done against you.

God is genuinely concerned about justice: "'Vengeance is mine, I will repay', says the Lord" (Romans 12:19). One day God will settle accounts with those who have injured others. We are not to take matters into our own hands. To the contrary, "if your enemy is hungry, feed him; if he is thirsty, give him something to drink; for by so doing you will heap burning coals on his head. Do not be overcome by evil but overcome evil with good" (Romans 12:20–21). Jesus said that if we want God to forgive us, we are to follow His example and forgive others from the heart (Matthew 18:35).

Overcoming Obstacles

Unfortunately, sometimes we may suffer as a result of our own unwise choices. Even so, our amazing God of grace is full of mercy, and like the father of the prodigal son, He runs to receive us back when we come to Him in repentance.

Resolving grief can become complicated if a widow struggles with unresolved feelings of fear, pain, anger, resentment, or guilt regarding her late spouse.

For example, the initial period of grief can be extended if a widow fears she can't live without her husband. It is normal to be challenged by her new circumstances, like taking on his jobs or living alone. Grief becomes paralyzing, however, if she is convinced that it would be impossible for her to learn to manage without him. She can learn to cope and find hope as she gradually begins to lean upon God, as her new Husband, in daily living.

A widow who has been the primary caregiver for her husband during an extended illness may feel relief when he dies. This relief may cause feelings of false guilt. The sudden lack for the need of intense caregiving is also a loss, leaving a void in her day. She may feel disoriented and even bored, not knowing what to do with herself or her time. She may not know what her purpose is after he passes away.

Sometimes a painful marriage can lead to resentment and, therefore, complicated grief after the spouse's passing. The widow may feel relieved because the constant turmoil of the relationship is gone. She may feel guilty for not experiencing the same level of sorrow that other widows seem to feel. One widow said that her husband provided financial and physical security, but he was unable to express emotions, such as empathy, mercy, or love. "When he passed away, I didn't even cry," she said.

Some widows may struggle with anger and resentment toward their husbands who died as a result of neglecting their own health. Or perhaps he died as a result of risky behavior. Or he may have died by suicide. In these cases, she may be mad, thinking that her husband chose to die and abandon her.

In any of these cases of complicated grief, the widow must first address her distressing emotions before she can move forward with the grief process. She may condemn herself for having feelings that are different than other widows, but when she realizes that God is for her, not against her, she can count on Him to help her untangle her emotions.

So, whether you are brand new to this experience of knowing God or have known him for many years, when troubles come, as they will for all of us, don't make the mistake of blaming God. Remember that He is FOR you. Turn toward, not away from Him. Psalm 46:1 says that He is our refuge and strength, our ever-present help in trouble. He truly WILL work ALL things together for our good.

Discussion Questions

1. The passing of time can give us a perspective on suffering that we do not have when we are in the middle of a situation. What do you see differently, now, that you didn't see previously?

_____

_____

_____

_____

_____

_____

_____

2. When we suffer unjustly, it can be tempting to retaliate. Jesus showed us a better way when He instructed us to turn the other cheek (Matthew 5:39). This is so contrary to human nature because we fear we will be injured further. In such cases, Jesus is our example. He said in John 10:18 regarding His own life, "No one takes it from me, but I lay it down of my own accord." This does not mean that we subject ourselves to abuse. It is important to take steps that are necessary to be safe. What it does mean is that we do not return evil for evil, but with blessing (1 Peter 3:9). How do these Scriptures apply to your grief journey?

_____

_____

_____

_____

_____

_____

_____

3. One reason it can be so difficult to return good for evil is that we fear justice will not be done. In such cases, 1 Peter 4:19 urges us to commit ourselves to our faithful Creator and continue to do good. We are to leave the injustice of the situation with God and trust that He will heal our souls. He will do a much better job than we ever could! If you are struggling with an unjust situation, such as an inheritance dispute or a family squabble, pause now and prayerfully commit this concern to the Lord. Do not hesitate to get professional help, if needed.

_____

_____

_____

_____

_____

_____

_____

_____

_____

Growing Stronger Guideline #10

DO NOT GRIEVE ALONE

Weep with those who weep until God, Himself,
wipes away all your tears.

CHAPTER TEN

DO NOT GRIEVE ALONE
TO COMFORT ALL WHO MOURN

*"The Spirit of the Lord is on me...to comfort all who mourn, and
provide for those who grieve in Zion—to bestow on them a crown
of beauty instead of ashes, the oil of gladness instead of mourning,
and a garment of praise instead of a spirit of despair"*
(Isaiah 61:2b–3).

I Know that God Sees Everything, but Does He Care?

God does care when we hurt. He knows that we need His help
when we grieve. God doesn't tell us to be brave and stop crying
when we are hurting. Instead, as a loving Father, He pays very close
attention to how we feel. Psalm 56:8 says, "You've kept track of my
every toss and turn through the sleepless nights, each tear entered
in your ledger, each ache written in Your book" (The Message).

Jesus Can Relate!

John 11 tells the story of three siblings, Mary, Martha, and
Lazarus who were close friends of Jesus. But just because they were
close to Jesus did not mean they would escape sorrow in this life.
While Jesus was in another town, Lazarus became deathly ill. Having
seen Jesus perform many miracles, Mary and Martha sent word
for Jesus to come and heal their brother. Jesus, knowing that He
intended to raise Lazarus back to life, purposely delayed until after
Lazarus had died.

When Jesus arrived, He was greeted by Lazarus' sisters and a
group of people in mourning. Even though He knew that the situation
was only temporary, He was very sad. He did not tell Mary, Martha,
and the rest of the mourners to stop crying, but empathized with
them and entered into their grief. John 11:33–36 tells us, "When
Jesus saw her (Mary) weeping, and the Jews who had come along
with her also weeping, He was deeply moved in spirit and troubled."
Jesus wept too.

Greg Laurie, in his book, *Hope for Hurting Hearts*, points out
that when Jesus was moved in spirit and troubled, the Greek word
for "troubled" could actually be translated as "angry." Why would
Jesus be sad when He knew He would raise Lazarus from the dead?
And why would Jesus be angry that Lazarus had died when He had
purposely stayed away long enough for Lazarus to go through the

dying process?

Jesus left Heaven and lived among us as a human. Hebrews 4:15 says that He is touched with the feeling of our weaknesses and infirmities. He is affected with the very same feelings that we feel when we encounter sickness and death, so He can have compassion on us. It is normal to feel sad and angry when someone we love is taken from us through death. Jesus is all God, and He is all man too! So, He also felt sad and angry at the death of His friend.

Jesus wasn't just an acquaintance. He loved and cared for Mary, Martha, and Lazarus as their Savior and their friend. They knew Jesus well as a human being and as their God. They knew the details of each others' lives.

Amazingly, in John 15:15, Jesus, the Son of God, says that He no longer calls us servants, but friends! He says that a servant does not know his master's business, but whatever He (Jesus) has received from the Father, He now has made known to us! He knows and cares about the details of our lives, and through the Holy Spirit in our hearts, we can know Him and His plans too!

Jesus was The Great Teacher. Here, Jesus was demonstrating how to be present with and love those who are grieving. He was showing us how to weep with those who weep. He was saying, "It is okay to be angry, to be sad, and to cry when you lose a loved one." He didn't rebuke Martha and Mary when they blamed Him for letting their brother die because of His absence. He also didn't jump to fix the situation before demonstrating that He understood and cared about their emotions.

Beyond the interactions with these sisters, Jesus was also communicating to men—everywhere and for all time—that it is alright for men to cry. Jesus knows that both men and women need to cry. Crying is a gift from God to help us release our heart's pain when it overflows. Crying does not make a man less manly. Jesus held the power of life and death in a single command, yet He openly allowed others to see His tender heart expressed through tears.

But once Jesus demonstrated His presence, love, and empathy, He didn't stop there! He proved that He IS the Resurrection and the Life by raising Lazarus from the dead! In doing so, Jesus not only gave Lazarus back his earthly life, but proved that Jesus is the One who holds the power over death!

If our husbands died believing in Christ, they will live eternally with Him. If a widow does not know whether her husband believed in Jesus or not, she can trust that God will be just and compassionate. One never knows a person's last thoughts. As Genesis 18:25 says,

"Shall not the Judge of all the earth do right?" The implied answer is "Yes!"

If our husbands died in faith, believing that they were going to be healed, we are left to wrestle with this question: "Why wasn't he healed?" We know that God could have healed him if He had so chosen. After all, Jeremiah 32:27 ESV says, "Behold, I am the Lord, the God of all flesh. Is there anything too hard for me?" God's ability is not the question.

A widow may ask, "Why didn't God want to heal my husband? Didn't He care about my husband? About me? About our children? Didn't we have enough faith? Didn't we pray enough?" Maybe she did pray. She did believe. She did have enough faith—and still God chose to take her husband. A widow may return to anger at God for allowing her husband to die. Wrestling with these issues is a normal part of the bargaining stage of grief.

The answer to the widow's questions lies *not* in the *ability* of God, but in His *character*. God is love. He is just. He is kind. He is trustworthy. God is a good God. God's ways are not our ways. His thoughts are not our thoughts. He has His reasons. And all His reasons are ultimately for our good and for His glory.

I (Mary Beth) wrestled with the fact that Bob and I had believed, up until Bob's final heartbeat, that God would heal him. As a family, we prayed and fasted, believing without doubt. We stood on the promises of God's Word. Hundreds of us joined in prayer for Bob. And still, Jesus took Bob home.

What happened?

I had no answer to this question. I chose to trust God. Months later, the Holy Spirit revealed to me that since Bob had died in faith believing, like the saints in Hebrews Chapter 11, God gave him a special reward when he arrived in Heaven. "These were all commended for their faith, yet none of them received what had been promised. God had planned something better for us so that only together with us would they be made perfect" (Hebrews 11:39-40).

How Does God Comfort Us?

God is love. God understands that we need comfort! Isaiah 53 shows how Jesus identifies with our grief. Here, He is called the "Man of Sorrows." It says that He was acquainted with grief. Not only did He take our sins upon the cross, but Isaiah goes on to say that He bore our grief and carried away our sorrows! He cares deeply when we are affected by the loss of a loved one, the loss of a dream, or something significant in our lives. He knows us better than anyone else and promises to comfort us just as a mother or father would comfort their hurting child. Isaiah 66:13 says, "As a mother comforts her child, so will I comfort you." Who can bring more consolation to a child than her mother? Yet, we also have a deep need for fatherly love. God has promised, "As a father has compassion on his children, so the Lord has compassion on those who fear Him; for He knows how we are formed, He remembers that we are dust" (Psalm 103:14).

Again, Jesus expressed motherly love when He said, "How often I have longed to gather your children together, as a hen gathers her chicks under her wings" (Matthew 23:37). Just like a mother hen, Jesus longs to cover us with His wings and bring us comfort and safety from the inevitable storms of life. Psalm 91:4 says, "He will cover you with his feathers, and under His wings you will find refuge; His faithfulness will be your shield and rampart."

Ultimately, God will personally wipe away every tear from our eyes. There will be no more death or mourning or crying or pain, for the old order of things (the world as we know it now) will have passed away (Revelation 21:4).

Don't Grieve Alone!

Just as Jesus wept with Mary and Martha, He knows that our painful journey of grief is not to be traveled alone. We need other people to come alongside us as we work through the emotions surrounding loss. Jesus did this with His friends. He will help us too! Grief is the process by which we let go of what we can't keep. Mourning is the outward expression of grief which brings our sorrow into relationship with God and others.

An important part of the ministry of Jesus is "to comfort all who mourn and to provide for those who grieve" (Isaiah 61:2–3a). Because we are the Body of Christ on this earth, we also have received the ministry of comforting others in their sorrow. People experiencing grief need the comfort of brothers and sisters in Christ. The "God of all comfort" consoles us, then "we can comfort those in any trouble with the comfort we ourselves have received from God. For just as the sufferings of Christ flow over into our lives, so also through Christ, our comfort overflows" (2 Corinthians 1:4–5).

This giving and receiving of comfort increases bonding and love between people. This is one of the reasons why Jesus said, "Blessed are those who mourn, for they will be comforted" (Matthew 5:4). Therefore, rather than telling someone, "don't cry," we can share in the compassion of Christ as we bring comfort to others. When we do this, we are fulfilling the scriptural command to "Rejoice with those who rejoice, and weep with those who weep" (Romans 12:15).

Will it Ever End?

When we are in the middle of grief, it can be hard to imagine that happy days will ever come again. Though it may not seem like it at the time, little by little, joy will return. While depression can come and sit like a gray cloud, the process of grief does have an end. Isaiah 57:18 says, "I have seen his ways, but I will heal him; I will guide him and restore comfort to him." Jeremiah 31:13 says, "I will turn their mourning into gladness; I will give them comfort and joy instead of sorrow."

Also, Jeremiah 31:3–4 says that the Lord loves us with an everlasting love and draws us with His unfailing kindness. Because of this, in time we will once again "go out to dance with the joyful."

We Do Not Grieve as Others Do

Though Christians are subject to the hardships and losses that come with living on planet Earth, we do not grieve as others who have no hope! Because Jesus died and rose again, we know that we too will rise to live forever in Heaven with Him! Although death causes great pain, Jesus' resurrection and our promise of eternal life takes away death's sting!

Testimony from Mary Beth

My father, Rev. John M. Baker, was a very special and beloved man. A Free Methodist pastor for over 50 years, he was highly esteemed by thousands of people. But to me, he was Daddy and my hero! He lived and loved in such a way as to exemplify the heart of my loving Heavenly Father.

When Dad passed away at age 80, family and friends flew in from all over the country to honor his life. Although my family grieved greatly, we discovered that death had lost its sting.

During the process of helping my mother with memorial arrangements, some of my family members, along with Mom and Dad's pastor, gathered at the funeral home in the room where Dad's body lay. It was now only a shell of the man that we all loved so much. His spirit was with Jesus! Yes, there were tears, but because we are also a very musical family, someone began to lead out in a song of worship. All of us, including my mother, the grieving widow, held hands and sang song after song of praise and thanks to God, many of which we had sung with our father (a *wonderful* tenor). We stopped singing only because we realized that we might have been too loud and joyful for the people who were visiting in other rooms! Then the pastor led the family in a very meaningful prayer before we each said our tender and tearful good-byes.

This type of rejoicing in the middle of sorrow is only possible through the power of the Holy Spirit and the knowledge that our loved one is now in the arms of Jesus!

Pass it On!

Because we do have hope and the comfort of the Holy Spirit, we can pass this comfort on to those around us who have also suffered loss. The following are a few practical suggestions to help others who are grieving:

1. Respond with a visit, a phone call, a card, or a letter. The mourner may especially treasure written notes for a long time. The Widows Project has greeting cards appropriate for special occasions in the widow's life such as her birthday, wedding anniversary, her husband's birthday and the anniversary of his passing. Please see thewidowsproject.org for details.
2. Don't worry if you don't know what to say. Many times, your very presence, a hug, or a shared tear is enough to express that you care. "Weep with those who weep" (Romans 12:15).
3. Reassure the mourner that grieving is a necessary part of her recovery.
4. Listen compassionately to the grieving widow as she expresses her thoughts and feelings. She may especially want to talk about her husband.
5. Don't be afraid to talk about the deceased loved one but share encouraging memories.
6. Don't say, "Let me know if there's anything I can do to help," but offer specific, practical assistance.
7. Remember that she will need support for months to come because grieving takes time.
8. Assure her of your prayer support during her grief.

Grief is a process with a beginning and an end. While things will never be the way they were before the loss, we will find a "new normal" and feel happiness and joy once again. Weeping may endure for the night season, but Psalm 30:5 assures us, "rejoicing comes in the morning!"

Discussion Questions

1. A Honduran proverb says, "Grief shared is half grief; joy shared is double joy." God knows that we need others when we are grieving, which is why Romans 12:15 says, "Rejoice with those who rejoice; mourn with those who mourn." What family, friends, ministers, or helpers are part of your grief support system? Who are the people who offered to help?

_____

_____

_____

_____

_____

_____

_____

_____

2. Consider joining a support group to process your grief. Christian support groups, such as The Widows Project and GriefShare, meet in many churches or Zoom groups. Secular grief groups can be helpful, but they do not offer hope in Jesus. Don't isolate, but be proactive and check the internet for grief groups that meet near you.

_____

_____

_____

_____

_____

_____

_____

3. Describe your pain and share it honestly with God now, and, when possible, with trusted friends. Remember, "Blessed are those who mourn, for they will be comforted" (Matthew 5:4).

_____

_____

_____

_____

_____

_____

_____

_____

4. In order to grieve in a healthy way, we need to understand what the loss involves. Each loss will have multiple levels. For example, losing a job involves not only the loss of income, but a secondary loss of the daily camaraderie of co-workers.

   The following is a huge assignment, so take it slowly, and, if at all possible, do it together with someone you trust. If you are currently suffering a loss or have a loss from the past that you have not worked through, first identify the primary loss, then list the secondary losses associated with it.

_____

_____

_____

_____

_____

_____

_____

_____

_____

Growing Stronger Guideline #11

Let Your Light Shine

Grow stronger through your loss
and become a blessing to others.

CHAPTER ELEVEN

LET YOUR LIGHT SHINE
YOUR TRANSFORMATION BRINGS GOD GLORY

"They will be called oaks of righteousness, a planting of the LORD for the display of His splendor" (Isaiah 61:3b).

God is The Gardener

Isaiah 61: 3b says that we will be called "Oaks of Righteousness." An "Oak of Righteousness?" Is that a compliment? Yes, it is! Like the wood of an oak tree, beautiful and functional, God will make us magnificent and strong women to be used by Him. What an honor to think that by allowing Jesus to live through me, I can become a planting of the Lord, a beautiful tree in His garden, which brings Him glory! Isaiah 61:11 describes God's garden: "For as the soil makes the sprout come up and a garden causes seeds to grow, so the Sovereign LORD will make righteousness and praise spring up before all nations."

Further, in John 15: 1 Jesus says, "I am the True Vine and my Father is the Gardener." In verse five, Jesus goes on to say that we are the branches in the True Vine, who is Jesus. He says that if we remain in Him and He remains in us, we will produce much fruit. We can't do anything without Him.

To produce an abundant crop of fruit, a skilled gardener will prune the branches. Without pruning, the spindly branches are unable to support the fruit. We have a choice. As widows, we can decide whether or not to abide in Him and accept His loving pruning. Jesus promises, "If you remain in Me and My Words remain in you, ask whatever you wish and it will be given you. This is to My Father's glory, that you bear much fruit, showing yourselves to be My disciples" (John 15: 7, 8). Our fruitful lives reflect the magnificence of the Gardener and His purposes in and through us.

God is The Potter!

In Isaiah 64:8, Isaiah describes God as a Potter. "Yet You, LORD, are our Father. We are the clay; You are the Potter; we are all the work of Your hand."

When a woman's husband dies, she may not be thrilled with the Potter's choice, but as Isaiah 29:16 questions, "How foolish can you be? He is the Potter, and He is certainly greater than you, the clay! Should the created thing say of the One who made it, 'He didn't make me'? Does a jar ever say, 'The potter who made me is stupid'?" (NLT). Or as the Message Bible states, "You have everything backward! You treat the Potter as a lump of clay. Does a book say to its author, 'He didn't write a word of me'? Does a meal say to the woman who cooked it, 'She had nothing to do with this'?"

How foolish it would be to respond to God in that way! So even though we may not appreciate the way He forms and reforms us, we can remind ourselves that God knows what He is doing. He truly does work everything together for our good (Romans 8:28). He re-creates us into a vessel which is even more valuable than the original.

"But how can I, a widow, be a beautiful and functional vessel?" you may ask. "I've been broken!"

In the art of mosaics, shattered pottery or china, which otherwise would have been discarded, is rearranged and transformed into uniquely beautiful and valuable works of art. When we yield to the Potter's design, the repaired mosaics of our lives are even more beautiful than if we had never been broken.

Years ago, at a ladies' retreat where Mary Beth led worship, a woman who had suffered much in a difficult marriage and with wayward children shared that during worship and prayer, God showed her a vision of her heart. It had been broken into many pieces. Then she saw the pieces of her heart put back together again—but this time, God had filled in between the broken places with pure gold! He had beautifully repaired her heart in a way that no one else could!

No Big Surprise!

Jesus warned us that we would have troubles in this world, but with God's help, as we grow through trials, we can become stronger than ever before. At some point, we will all suffer loss. Then we can choose how we will respond to grief. Some people blame God and turn their backs on Him when suffering comes. Instead of growing through adversity, they become bitter and resentful. This is a dangerous posture because God resists the proud, but gives grace to the humble (James 4: 6). But God has a better plan for us. Rather than accusing God, 1 Peter 5: 6-11 shows us God's path from humility to victory:

Humble yourselves, therefore, under God's mighty hand, that He may lift you up in due time. Cast all your anxiety on Him because He cares for you. Be self-controlled and alert. Your enemy the devil prowls around like a roaring lion looking for someone to devour. Resist him, stand firm in the faith, because you know that your brothers throughout the world are undergoing the same kind of sufferings.

And the God of all grace, who called you to His eternal glory in Christ, after you have suffered a little while, will Himself restore you and make you strong, firm and steadfast. To Him be the power for ever and ever. Amen.

The devil also has a plan for widows. He has no compassion. An opportunistic criminal, he targets the widow in her vulnerability. Self-defense experts teach that a villain needs three basic elements to commit a crime:

- the desire to commit a crime
- the ability to commit a crime
- the opportunity to commit a crime

While we cannot control a culprit's desire and ability to assault us, we can protect ourselves by not affording him an opportunity. God has provided Christians with ways to defend ourselves from the enemy. Not only is the devil a criminal, he is a coward. James 4:7 instructs us to "...submit to God. Resist the devil and he will flee from you."

God also freely gives us His armor to put on daily. Ephesians 6: 10-18 advises us about its use.

Finally, be strong in the Lord and in His mighty power. Put on the full armor of God so you can take your stand against the devil's schemes. For our struggle is not against flesh and blood, but against the rulers, against the authorities, against the powers of this dark world and against the spiritual forces of evil in the heavenly realms. Therefore, put on the full armor of God, so that when the day of evil comes, you may be able to stand your ground, and after you have done everything, to stand. Stand firm then. With the belt of truth buckled around your waist, with the breastplate of righteousness in place, and with your feet fitted with the readiness that comes from the Gospel of Peace. In addition to all this, take up the shield of faith, with which you can extinguish all the flaming arrows of the evil one. Take up the helmet of salvation and the sword of the Spirit, which is the Word of God. And pray in the Spirit on all occasions with all kinds of prayers and requests. With this in mind, be alert and always keep on praying for all the saints.

So, as we encounter troubles in this world, we can choose to:

- humble ourselves and not blame God,
- arm ourselves and resist the devil, and
- prepare ourselves and adopt God's view of suffering.

The Apostle Peter wrote in 1 Peter 4:12–16, 19, "Dear friends, do not be surprised at the fiery ordeal that has come on you to test you, as though something strange were happening to you. But rejoice inasmuch as you participate in the sufferings of Christ, so that you may be overjoyed when His glory is revealed." So according to Peter, we can face trials with a winning attitude when we remember to:

- not be surprised,
- rejoice to participate in the sufferings of Christ, and
- be overjoyed when Jesus' glory is revealed.

You are the Light of the World

When we suffer yet continue to do good, we bring glory to God. As a candle inside a broken pot beams through the cracks, so we widows can shine for Jesus, even in our brokenness. In Matthew 5:14–16, Jesus said,

You are the light of the world. A city on a hill cannot be hidden. Neither do people light a lamp and put it under a bowl. Instead, they put it on a stand, and it gives light to everyone in the house. In the same way, let your light shine before men, that they may see your good deeds and praise your Father in Heaven.

But what does it mean to let your light shine for Jesus? Just as the moon reflects the greater light of the sun, Christians reflect the glory of The Son. So let your light shine, not so that people will see how wonderful *you* are, but so they will see, through your good works, how wonderful *God* is! As we spend time with Him through the Word, prayer, and fellowship, we will become more and more like Christ. We will "all reflect the Lord's glory" as we "are being transformed into His likeness with ever-increasing glory, which comes from the Lord, who is the Spirit" (2 Corinthians 3:18). We can shine for Jesus even in the darkest moments of our lives.

Discussion Questions

1. Describe people from the Bible who were transformed after being broken and became displays of God's splendor. What were they like "before" and "after"?

_____

_____

_____

_____

_____

_____

_____

_____

_____

_____

2. Have you, or anyone you know, gone through this transformation process? If so, please share the "before" and "after" story.

_____

_____

_____

_____

_____

_____

_____

_____

_____

3. In the middle of your grief, remember that God has invested the very life of His Son, on your behalf, to bring you through to the other side. This is not only for your encouragement, but also for His glory! Reconsider Romans 8:32, "He who did not spare His own Son, but gave Him up for us all—how will He not also, along with Him, graciously give us all things?" Take a moment to thank God for His sacrifice of Jesus Christ, then ask Him specifically for the help that you need.

_____

_____

_____

_____

_____

_____

_____

_____

_____

_____

_____

_____

_____

_____

_____

_____

_____

_____

_____

_____

_____

_____

Growing Stronger Guideline #12

INVEST IN THE FUTURE

When you glorify God through your grief, you become
an example that will encourage generations to come.

CHAPTER TWELVE
INVEST IN THE FUTURE
REBUILDING THE GENERATIONS

"They will rebuild the ancient ruins and restore the places long devastated; they will renew the ruined cities that have been devastated for generations" (Isaiah 61:4).

Ruins Restored, Devastation Renewed

God is a Master Builder—and Rebuilder—even if the devastation has stood for many generations. The book of Nehemiah is a partial fulfillment of Isaiah 61:4, where God's people, led by Nehemiah, rebuilt the rubble of Jerusalem's walls.

Instead of ruin and devastation, shame and disgrace, God promises a double blessing to those who belong to Him. Not only are we blessed, but we can expect our children and their children to receive His blessing as well: "Their descendants will be known among the nations and their offspring among the peoples. All who see them will acknowledge that they are a people the LORD has blessed" (Isaiah 61:7). God promises to bless the children of those who belong to Him.

A widow will grieve the loss of her children's father, but her children will grieve their losses differently. Each child will miss their father uniquely because each had their own relationship with him. Even her husband's friends had their own relationship with her husband, and they won't grieve like she does.

For Generations to Come

How do you want to be remembered? Have you thought about it? Whether or not we are aware of it, we are making an impact on those around us. So why not live purposefully with future generations in mind?

As I (Dr. Meier) learned in medical school, "See One, Do One, Teach One." I first learned by watching my professors and other experienced doctors, then practiced with them nearby, and then helped other medical students by assisting them with what I had learned. The same principle can apply as we work our way through grief. With God's help and using the Guidelines in this book, we emerge from difficulties stronger than we ever were before. But let's not stop there! We can then pass on the principles we have learned from our own struggles to help our children, our friends, and significant others to grow from the wisdom we have gained. In this way, they will be better equipped to resolve future losses which inevitably crop up for all of us.

When our (Mary Beth's) kids were young, we taught them about tithing by giving them three little cups in which to divide their money. One was labeled, "GOD," the second, "SAVE," and the third, "SPEND." Recently, when babysitting our son David's children, I was delighted to see three cups labeled—you guessed it—"GOD," "SAVE," and "SPEND."

Some lessons, like this, are specifically taught. Others are simply caught in the process of daily living. Still others may not "sink in" until our grown kids have children of their own. What lessons do you want to pass on to the next generation?

The Most Important Lesson

Of course, the most important thing we can teach the next generation is how to become a Christian! We have come full circle! We must always put first things first. As Paul said in Acts 16:31, "Believe in the Lord Jesus, and you will be saved—you and your household." What good would it do to teach them about this life and ignore the eternal life to come? None! As Joel 1:3 reminds us, "Tell it to your children, and let your children tell it to their children, and their children to the next generation."

Set an Example

Not only do we share the Gospel with the next generation, but we can live a godly life that will encourage them long after we are gone. Though we may not be aware of it, today's events may be retold by our children, grandchildren, and even great grandchildren yet unborn! What kind of memories do you want to leave? Whether you have biological children or not, faith in Christ, passed through spiritual children, can greatly impact even more than "us four!" For example, Carmen Harris-Taylor, godmother of Mary Beth's children, will have many children in Heaven because of the people she has loved, served, and led to faith in Christ all around the world.

In 2003, I attended a prayer meeting where a wonderful lady, named Fran Lance prayed for my son Steve and me. Since the prayer was recorded, I was able to transcribe it. Fran did not know me well. I am amazed now at the Lord's timing! Look at the wonderful encouragement that the Lord gave me as Fran prayed:

Father, we just bless your daughter now in Jesus' name. Thank You, Lord. The Lord gives me Job 13:15, 'Though He slay me, yet will I hope in Him.' I just see you; you've pulled out all the stops. 'I'm going to follow the Lord no matter what.'

Life has not gone the way you thought it would. The Lord says, 'You have rolled with the punches.' I see you in a boxing ring and you've learned to dodge the blow of a punch. These punches are not from the Lord. He wants you to know that. Sometimes people think, 'The Lord's punishing me.' But the Lord says, 'Daughter, I love you so much.' And no way, no way would He ever, ever cause a battering of any kind, any sort, any punch of life. But He has given man free will, and man's free will has battered you.

But the Lord says, 'Daughter, I have brought gold out of you through it all.' Job 23:1, 'But He knows the way that I take. When He has tested me, I will come forth as gold. My feet have closely followed His steps; I have kept His way without turning aside. I have not departed from the commands of His lips. I have treasured the words of His mouth more than my daily bread.'

And that's how the Lord sees you. And you're coming forth as gold. Gold is refined in the fire. So, you didn't settle for the silver. Silver doesn't take as much heat as gold, but you said, 'Lord, I want to go for it. I don't want to just have this silver.' You're going for it.

Psalm 78:3, 'What we have heard and known, what our fathers have told us we will not hide them from their children. We will tell the next generation.' The Lord is saying that as you teach your child, it's going to go on to the next generation too, even the next and the next. So, verse 6, 'So the next generation would know them, even the children yet to be born. And they, in turn, would tell their children, and then they would put their trust in God.' So, as you put your life into your son or children, the Lord says, 'It will go on to the next generation, even to those unborn, yet.'

Thank You, Lord. We just bless Your daughter. We thank You, Lord, for just healing her wounded heart. And we thank You that You are the Healer. The Bible says that the Lord is close to those who are wounded, brokenhearted. Psalm 147:3-5: 'He heals the brokenhearted and binds up their wounds. He determines the number of stars and calls them each by name. Great is our Lord and mighty in power. His understanding has no limits.' We bless her in Jesus' name. Amen.

As you can imagine, this was a great blessing and tremendous encouragement! If you also have been refined by fire, dear widow, I would like to share this prayer blessing with you! Please take this prayer of encouragement and pray it as your own!

Little Ones to Him Belong

God cares about our suffering. He watches over us and helps us in the recovery process. But little eyes are watching too! Let's honor God, even in our grief recovery, so that those who follow will have an example to cheer them on when they face the inevitable losses of life. Of course, we would love to spare our children and grandchildren from trials, but our prayers and example can follow them long after we are gone.

In this world, we all suffer. It is just the nature of life. But Jesus told us not to be worried about this because He is preparing a place in Heaven for those who believe in Him. We're going to live in the Father's House forever! It's all good there! In John 14:1–3 Jesus said,

Do not let your hearts be troubled. You believe in God; believe also in me. My Father's house has many rooms; if that were not so, would I have told you that I am going there to prepare a place for you? And if I go and prepare a place for you, I will come back and take you to be with me that you also may be where I am.

The Cloud of Witnesses

Hebrews Chapter 12 begins with these now-familiar verses: "Therefore, since we are surrounded by such a great cloud of witnesses, let us throw off everything that hinders and the sin that so easily entangles. And let us run with perseverance the race marked out for us." Our husbands, family and friends who have died in Christ are among those in that cloud of witnesses who are watching us run and cheering us on!

This great cloud includes those who have gone before us, as well as those who will come after us! Our faith-filled journey through grief can give courage to our children, grandchildren, and those yet unborn. Our God-empowered lives can teach those who follow us— even many generations after we are gone—to persevere through their own trials and do great things for God!

Children are Our Arrows!

When I (Mary Beth) was nineteen years old and feeling sad from a major disappointment, my very wise father comforted me with this thought: "When an archer shoots an arrow, the farther back he pulls the bow, the farther the arrow will travel." Although I didn't really understand it at the time, I now see that as Christians we can yield to the Archer who will take what seems to be a setback and use it to "shoot us" farther than we ever would have gone had that setback not occurred.

Psalm 127:4–5 says that children are a reward and a heritage from the Lord. It goes on to say that they are like arrows in the hand of a warrior. As women warriors in a spiritual battle, through our prayers and godly example we can shoot the "arrows" of our biological and spiritual children far into the future to win battles for God's Kingdom!

In the same way, the sacrifices of our sufferings for Jesus will bear much fruit, not only in our lifetime, but as following generations take courage from our example, they will serve to advance the kingdom of God, bearing 30, 60, and even 100 times more fruit!

Next Generation Blessing

We would like to end this book with a Next Generation Blessing Prayer. Please feel free to personalize this prayer for your biological and/or spiritual children, grandchildren, and those yet to be born!

Dear Father,
We pray a blessing on the generations to follow us. We pray that they will come to know You at a very young age. We pray they will love You and serve You all the days of their lives. We pray that they will grow in wisdom and stature and favor with God and man, just like Jesus did.

We pray that they will tell the next generation of Your praiseworthy deeds, Your power, and the wonders You have done. We pray that they would teach their children Your mighty acts, so the next generation would know about them, even the children yet to be born, and they in turn would tell their children. We pray that they would put their trust in You and would not forget Your deeds but keep your commands.

We pray that when they face trials in life, they will remember that the sufferings they experience in this life are nothing compared to the glory that will be revealed in the next one. We pray that they will stand side by side with us in Heaven praising You for the way that You brought us through, all the while changing us from glory to glory. And we pray that they will not come alone, but through faith in Christ, will bring many untold numbers of people to Heaven with them.

In Jesus' name, Amen.

Discussion Questions

1. God's plan is for our children to have a life of blessing and peace, as Isaiah 54:13 says, "All your sons will be taught by the LORD, and great will be your children's peace." If there are areas where your children are not enjoying this peace right now, take a minute to describe this to the Lord and ask Him for the peace He has promised.

_____

_____

_____

_____

_____

_____

_____

_____

2. Proverbs 13:22 says, "A good man leaves an inheritance to his children's children." In this case, we are not just referring to a material inheritance, but a legacy of godliness which will bless generations after us, even those who are yet to be born! It's amazing to think about the impact of our daily lives on so many others. Reflect on what your parents and grandparents have passed on to you. What do you want to pass on to your children and grandchildren?

_____

_____

_____

_____

_____

_____

_____

_____

3. What about the legacy of those who have never had children? How can they leave an inheritance to the generations to come? Godly women through the years have instructed generations with their lives. Consider women like Mother Teresa of Calcutta, Helen Keller, and Corrie ten Boom who have impacted and mentored millions by their examples of integrity, courage, love, and generosity. If you are not a parent at this time, how would you like to live your life in such a way as to impact future generations?

---

4. Although we admire heroes of the faith in our culture, none of them were perfect! We do not have to live perfect lives to impact those who follow us. In fact, some of us may best glorify God by telling of His wonderful forgiveness and restoration in our lives, or how He saved us from calamity and disaster. Consider writing a letter to your children, grandchildren, or others your life may have touched, and tell them what God has done to help you through the loss of your husband. What is the legacy you would most want to impart to them?

Twelve Growing Stronger Guidelines

1. **Keep First Things First.** Develop an intimate relationship with Jesus, the true Higher Power because you are powerless to overcome crises in your own strength, alone. "The Spirit of the Sovereign Lord is on me, because the Lord has anointed me to preach good news to the poor" (Isaiah 61:1).
2. **Don't Suffer Alone.** Give your broken heart to God and his people to receive healing from both. "The Spirit of the Sovereign Lord is on me... He has sent me to bind up the brokenhearted" (Isaiah 61:1).
3. **Confession Leads to Freedom.** To become truly free from bondage and truly healed, you must confess your own sins and flaws to safe, significant others as well as to Jesus. "The Spirit of the Sovereign Lord is on me... to proclaim freedom for the captives and release from darkness for the prisoners" (Isaiah 61:1).
4. **With God's Help, Get Rid of It.** Lay aside the things that are holding you back. "Therefore, since we are surrounded by such a great cloud of witnesses, let us throw off everything that hinders and the sin that so easily entangles, and let us run with perseverance the race marked out for us" (Hebrews 12:1).
5. **Keep Looking Up.** Make PERSONAL GROWTH an even higher priority than resolving your current crisis. "Let us fix our eyes on Jesus, the author and perfecter of our faith" (Hebrews 12:2a).
6. **Hang In There.** Whenever you feel like giving up, endure. "Jesus... who for the joy set before Him endured the cross, scorning its shame, and sat down at the right hand of the throne of God" (Hebrews 12:2b).
7. **Don't Lose Heart.** When you experience discipline, remind yourself that God is a good Father and say, "My Abba (Daddy) Father loves me." "Moreover, we have all had human fathers who disciplined us and we respected them for it. How much more should we submit to the Father of our spirits and live!" (Hebrews 12:10).
8. **Don't Grow Weary.** Remember that your victory is just around the corner. "Therefore, strengthen your feeble arms and weak knees. Make level paths for your feet, so that the lame may not be disabled, but rather healed" (Hebrews 12:12–13).

9. **Remember That God is On Your Side.** God's love is not based on your performance, but on His goodness. "The Spirit of the Lord is on me...to proclaim the year of the Lord's favor and the day of vengeance of our God" (Isaiah 61:2).

10. **Do Not Grieve Alone**. Weep with those who weep until God, himself, wipes away all your tears. "The Spirit of the Lord is on me...to comfort all who mourn, and provide for those who grieve in Zion—to bestow on them a crown of beauty instead of ashes, the oil of gladness instead of mourning, and a garment of praise instead of a spirit of despair" (Isaiah 61:2b–3).

11. **Let Your Light Shine.** Allow your crisis to grow you stronger and MORE equipped to be a blessing to others. "They will be called oaks of righteousness, a planting of the Lord for the display of His splendor" (Isaiah 61:3b).

12. **Invest in the Future**. When you overcome crises with God's help, you become an example that will encourage generations to come. "They will rebuild the ancient ruins and restore the places long devastated; they will renew the ruined cities that have been devastated for generations" (Isaiah 61:4).

Supplemental Reading for Widows

Aldrich, Sandra P.
Will I ever Be Whole Again?:
Surviving the Death of Someone You Love

Burke, John
Imagine Heaven

Calligaro, Julie A.
The Widow's Resource:
How to Solve the Financial and Legal Problems
that Occur within Six to Nine Months of Your Husband's Death

Cornish, Carol
The Undistracted Widow:
Serving God after Losing your Husband

Davis, Verdell
Let Me Grieve but Not Forever

Feinberg, Linda
I'm Grieving as Fast as I Can:
How Young Widows and Widowers Can Cope and Heal

Felber, Marta
Finding your Way after Your Spouse Dies
(many resources in back of book)

Ginsburg, Genevieve Davis
Widow to Widow:
Thoughtful, Practical Ideas for Rebuilding Your Life:
Challenges, Changes, Decision-making and Relationships

GriefShare
Through a Season of Grief:
Devotions for your Journey from Mourning to Joy

Groves, Elizabeth W. D.
Becoming a Widow:
The Ache of Missing Your Other Half

Haugk, Kenneth C.
Finding Hope and Healing:
Journeying through Grief series, Book 3

Lyons, Christine, and Schaefer, Dan
How do we Tell the Children?:
A Step-by-Step Guide for Helping Children
Two to Teen Cope when Someone Dies

Mabry, Richard L.
The Tender Scar

Morrell, Ben with Lisa Morrell
Greatly, Deeply
(Written by a member of Seattle Widows)

Neff, Miriam
From One Widow to Another

Pappas, Kristine
Widow for a Season:
Finding Your Identity in Christ

Pink, Arthur W.
Comfort for Christians

Rogers, Joyce
Grace for the Widow:
A Journey through the Fog of Loss

Sissom, Ruth
Instantly a Widow

Sittser, Jerry
A Grace Disguised

Wright, H. Norman
Reflections of a Grieving Spouse

Zonnebelt-Smeege, Susan J.
Getting to the Other Side:
Overcoming the Loss of a Spouse

How to Find a Great Therapist

By Mary Beth Woll, MA, LMHC

"Wait a second! Find a therapist?!? Do I need therapy? With a little willpower, I could handle this on my own, right?"

The truth is, everybody needs counsel, at one time or another, from loved ones, trusted family and friends, pastors, mentors, and professionals. Taking this important step could save a person's life and potentially change the course of many generations to come!

Before beginning the search for a therapist, it is good to clearly define the need.

- What are my symptoms?
- Is there an immediate threat to someone's safety?
- Is there a desire to include spirituality in therapy?
- Will it be individual, group, or family therapy?
- Is there a need for a specialist in treating such cases as Bipolar Disorder, Post Traumatic Stress Disorder, and others?
- How will I pay for it? Can I use my insurance? (Currently, children are covered under their parent's insurance until age 26, even if married.) Do they offer a sliding scale?
- Would a support group or peer counseling provide what I need or do I need a professional who specializes in my situation?

With all these questions, is it any wonder that many people never make it to the therapist's door? There are good answers to all these questions, but even before answering them, there are often other roadblocks that need to be addressed, like how does one even know when it's time to see a professional?

How can I determine if I need therapy?

Consider when a person catches a cold. If they are sensible, they will drink more fluids and get more rest. If the cold persists, they may take vitamins or over-the-counter cold remedies. If the cold develops into bronchitis or pneumonia, it's time to see a doctor! In such cases, it would be unwise and potentially life-threatening, to continue to self-treat or self-medicate.

In the same way, it is important to recognize when emotional, behavioral, or soul needs are too much for one's personal support system. That's when it's time to stop "white-knuckling it" and get professional help!

As a Christian, shouldn't I just rely on my church and my faith instead of a counselor?

Sometimes a person's faith background or the religious traditions they were brought up with can be a roadblock toward counseling. Many have been taught that if their faith is strong enough, they need not rely on outside counseling. Some wonder, "Is it even okay for a Christian to go to therapy? If I were a 'better Christian', I wouldn't need therapy, right? Shouldn't I just read my Bible and pray more?"

This kind of thinking can prolong a person's pain and unnecessarily add to the shame they may already be experiencing. If someone is dealing with past trauma or abuse, some kind of addiction, or any number of other mental health challenges, a trained counselor can be an incredible tool and ally. In these cases, telling them, "You don't need counseling. Just become a better, stronger Christian," or "Just read the Bible and pray more," can condemn them to more years of symptoms, hiding, and unhealthy coping strategies instead of being helpful. In a loving community of faith, we really should be encouraging each other to seek out the help we need, and receiving help from a trained counselor is a wonderful and healthy avenue.

What about medication?

Sometimes, there is a very real and legitimate need for medication in treatment for depression, anxiety, and bipolar disorder, among others. This must not be minimized any more than one would advise a diabetic not to take their insulin! Often people struggle with the idea of starting on medication, thinking that it makes them seem weak or even "crazy." The reality is that the brain is an organ, like any other part of the body, which can become sick. In some cases, the brain is formed a little differently from birth and requires medical support.

Many Christians, and particularly those who have overcome drug addiction, struggle with medication issues, thinking that a "better Christian" would not need an antidepressant or mood stabilizer. This misconception can keep many people away from much needed treatment. Of course, it is true that God still heals, but apparently, He also chooses to use medicine and does not condemn us for it. Jesus confirmed this when He said in Matthew 9:12, "It is not those who are healthy who need a physician, but those who are sick." Praying for the sick is a vital ministry of the church, but it is just as dangerous for the church to advise against medicine as it would be for pastors and church members to line up and write out prescriptions for each other on Sunday mornings! This calls for a mental health professional.

Although therapists do not prescribe medicine, they can diagnose and refer for proper medical treatment, which is most effective in conjunction with therapy.

Is my past affecting my current life and relationships?

Some people experience childhood sexual abuse or other trauma that is terrifying or impossible for a child to understand. Memories of such horror don't go away. They are so threatening that the mind could protect the person by locking these memories away in the subconscious for years while the person carries on with the business of growing up. Later, these memories can present as unexplained behavioral symptoms or big blank blocks of time in their childhood memories. When these symptoms begin to emerge in adult years, the person may need someone who can help them articulate and resolve what was previously unspeakable.

When they are ready to face the pain of the past, it is not safe or appropriate to talk to just anyone, although friends and family may play a part in the healing process. It is important that they seek out someone who is trained and skilled in such work; otherwise, it is possible for the unequipped helper to inflict more damage in the process.

How can counseling help my relationships?

In addition to depression, anxiety, and posttraumatic symptoms, relationships may become so conflicted or distant that a third party's perspective and input is needed. Such situations can be overwhelming to a widow's support system of friends and family. Once again, professional help is in order. Seeking counseling, in such cases, is actually the responsible thing to do in order to continue to function well in the family and on the job.

What type of therapist is best for me?

Some of the confusion in finding a great therapist can be found in the titles alone.

- Psychiatrists will usually be identified as "Dr." with "MD" following their name. These medical doctors specialize in the diagnosis and treatment of mental or psychiatric illnesses. They are trained in counseling, but typically use the client's report of symptoms to prescribe appropriate medications and refer clients to therapists for counseling. While it is true that family practice doctors prescribe the overwhelming proportion of antidepressants in the United States, I prefer to recommend a psychiatrist when medication is needed, because, as specialists, they can often catch a subtle need that can make a big difference in prescribing the right medication.

- Psychologists (PhD or PsyD) have a doctoral degree in Psychology. They are specialists in various methods of therapy, as well as psychological testing. Psychologists do not prescribe medications but can refer to a psychiatrist, if necessary.
- Licensed Mental Health Counselors (LMHC, LCPC) have a Master's Degree in Psychology, plus 3,000 hours of post-master's experience in order to be licensed. They are therapists who can diagnose and treat a wide range of problems including depression, anxiety, bipolar disorder, post-traumatic stress disorder (PTSD), sexual abuse, ADD/ADHD, grief, suicidal impulses, addiction, substance abuse, stress management, self-esteem issues, emotional health and family, parenting and marital issues. In addition to individuals, they can treat couples and families. They do not prescribe medications but can refer to a psychiatrist.
- Licensed Marriage and Family Therapists, (LMFT) are therapists with a Master's Degree in Psychology and post-master's experience (similar to the Licensed Mental Health Counselor) but with more specialized training in issues regarding marriage and family. They can also treat all the issues listed above.
- Licensed Social Workers (MSW, LCSW) also have a Master's Degree in Social Work and post-master's experience. They specialize in providing services to help their clients' psychological and social functioning. Social workers can also treat the above therapy issues. In addition, they are specially trained to provide counseling and resources to help a person better function in their environment and relationships.
- Pastoral Counselors (Rev., M Div, Pastor) are usually licensed or ordained ministers who also have training in counseling. Their emphasis tends to focus on biblical principles, spiritual formation and direction, and improving relationships. It is important to note that, depending on how or where the Pastor was ordained, they may not have been required to have any training in counseling at all. It is dangerous to assume that just because someone is a Pastor, they are

equipped to counsel you in areas of mental health.

(NOTE: States have similar licenses but may use different license names/initials and may have different requirements. For example, a Licensed Mental Health Counselor (LMHC) in the State of Washington is similar to a Licensed Clinical Professional Counselor (LCPC) in the State of Illinois, but there may be some differences. Don't hesitate to ask for clarification of the initials or degree of a professional when scheduling to see them.)

How can I determine I've found the right therapist for me?

In an effort to answer some of these concerns, I will share how I found my own therapist. Yes, therapists need therapists too! We all have injuries in life. The better healed I am, the better therapist I will be. Experiencing the process also gives me empathy for my clients who are undergoing this process.

Here are the things that were important to me as I looked for a therapist:

- **Covered**: She was listed on my insurance plan.
- **Competence**: She went to a respected university and has a good work history.
- **Conviction**: There are certain moral principles which are non-negotiable for me. I didn't want to wrestle with these issues during therapy, but needed someone who shared this baseline with me so they would be better able to advise me. Since my faith informs my decisions, choosing a therapist who was also a Christian was THE most important aspect for me.
- **Compassion**: I found that she is a very caring individual. This is also critical for me. If I felt that the therapist didn't really care, I would go elsewhere.
- **Connection**: She and I "hit it off." This makes therapy so much more pleasant
- **Consistency**: She is dependable and reliable. I know what to expect when I go to therapy.
- **Convenience**: Her office is within about a half hour commute. I was willing to travel this distance for a great therapist.

Finding a great therapist has been a huge benefit in my own life. Hopefully, these thoughts will also help you navigate the maze of finding a therapist who is a good fit for you. As a counselor, I know that I have the opportunity to change lives daily! Sometimes, like braces, it is slow and incremental. Other times, like heart surgery, it is critical and immediate. Still for others it is like physical therapy — just plain hard work, long-term, and endurance-building.

It takes courage to begin the counseling process. Often, we will experience resistance from within ourselves and from others. This is normal and to be expected. But the rewards are well worth the risk as these life changes can be deep, permanent, and enriching not only for you, but for your loved ones. And even one changed life can change the course of events for generations yet to come!

Bibliography

Anne Sullivan Biography. n.d. http://www.biography.com/people/anne-sullivan-9498826#teaching-helen-keller (accessed April 20, 2014).

Harriet Tubman Biography. n.d. http://www.biography.com/people/harriet-tubman-9511430 (accessed October 31, 2014).

Helen Keller Biography. n.d. http://www.biography.com/people/helen-keller-9361967#synopsis (accessed April 20, 2014).

Helen Keller Foundation. n.d. http://www.helenkellerfoundation.org/helen-keller/ (accessed April 29, 2014).

Henry, Matthew. *The Blue Letter Bible, Matthew Henry Commentary.* n.d. https://www.blueletterbible.org/Comm/mhc/Rev/Rev_002.cfm (accessed October 31, 2014).

Holmes, Leonard. *How the "Widowhood Effect" Puts Widows at Risk After a Spouse's Death.* n.d. http://www.verywellmind.com (accessed October 21, 2020).

Keller, Helen. *The Story of My Life .* n.d. http://www.afb.org/mylife/book.asp?ch=P1Ch6 (accessed November 1 , 2014).

Liddell, Eric. *The Eric Liddell Centre .* n.d. http://www.ericliddell.org/ericliddell/home (accessed October 31, 2014).

Lucado, Max. *God Thinks You're Wonderful.* Nashville: Thomas Nelson , 2003.

Woll, Mary Beth; Meier, MD, Paul. *Growing Stronger: 12 Guidelines to Turn Your Darkest Hour into Your Greatest Victory.* New York: Morgan James Publishing, 2015.

Wright, Rolland. *The Widows Project: Serving the Widowed with the Father's Heart.* Everett: The Widows Project, 2019.

About the Authors

Mary Beth Woll, MA, LMHC
Mary Beth Woll was married to Bob for almost 39 years before the Lord took him home. Bob and Mary Beth were co-music ministers for 20 years. Together they have four children and eight grandchildren. Mary Beth has a master's degree in counseling/psychology and works as a therapist with Meier Clinics. She also co-authored a book with Paul Meier, M.D., *"Growing Stronger: 12 Guidelines to Turn Your Darkest Hour into your Greatest Victory."*

Linda Smith

Linda Smith was married to Kirby for 37 years, and they have two children and six grandchildren. She comes from a background in education – both Christian and secular. She has taught at every age level and has led several widows' support groups since becoming a widow in 2013.

Paul Meier, M.D.

Paul Meier, M.D. is a psychiatrist and founder of the national chain of Meier Clinics. He is also the author of more than 90 books that have sold over seven million copies in more than 30 languages.

www.meierclinics.com

Next Generation Blessing

Dear Father,
We pray a blessing on the generations to follow us. We pray that they will come to know You at a very young age. We pray they will love You and serve You all the days of their lives. We pray that they will grow in wisdom and stature and favor with God and man, just like Jesus did.

We pray that they will tell the next generation of Your praiseworthy deeds, Your power, and the wonders You have done. We pray that they would teach their children Your mighty acts, so the next generation would know about them, even the children yet to be born, and they in turn would tell their children. We pray that they would put their trust in You and would not forget Your deeds but keep your commands.

We pray that when they face trials in life, they will remember that the sufferings they experience in this life are nothing compared to the glory that will be revealed in the next one. We pray that they will stand side by side with us in Heaven praising You for the way that You brought us through, all the while changing us from glory to glory. And we pray that they will not come alone, but through faith in Christ, will bring many untold numbers of people to Heaven with them.

In Jesus' name, Amen.